Advancing Social Development

A World Bank Contribution
to the Social Summit

The World Bank
Washington, D.C.

Published March 1995 by The International Bank for Reconstruction and Development/THE WORLD BANK
1818 H Street, N.W.
Washington, D.C. 20433

First printing March 1995
Second printing June 1995

ISBN 0-8213-3208-2

Cover photographs: Curt Carnemark, World Bank

Contents

Boxes

Figures

Foreword

BY ANY SENSIBLE MEASURE, THE DEVELOPMENT EXPERIENCE of the past forty years has been an astonishing success: life expectancy and education levels have increased dramatically, and average per capita incomes in the developing world have doubled.

Still, much remains to be done. Over one billion people worldwide struggle to survive on less than one dollar a day, too many infants and children still die from malnutrition and preventable diseases, and large numbers of people are unemployed or locked into low-productivity work. Compounding the problems of poverty and unemployment is the threat of social disintegration, manifested in the crime, violence, conflict, and war that have cost millions of lives.

In response to these global problems, the United Nations called a World Summit for Social Development to address three related challenges: poverty reduction, employment generation, and social integration. The Summit will bring together heads of state, researchers, and representatives of international agencies and nongovernmental organizations to lay the foundation for people-oriented economic and social progress. To aid the deliberations, World Bank staff have prepared this paper, focusing on some crucial issues of economic and social development and on the World Bank's support for country efforts to address these issues. The judgments in the paper do not necessarily reflect the views of the Board of Directors of the World Bank or the governments they represent.

Although there is no blueprint for development, there are clear lessons from country experience on how to achieve sustained improvements in incomes, employment, and social indicators. Governments have a critical role to play, for only they can create an environment that allows private enterprise to flourish and civil society to thrive. Central to this are sound economic policies. Many countries are embarked on the arduous task of economic reform; to reap the benefits, they must persevere in these efforts, making sure that appropriate safety nets are provided for the poor. Equally essential are investments in people—to develop the human capital that people need to increase their productivity, to rise out of poverty, and to lead fuller lives as informed and active citizens.

Promoting economic and social development is at the core of the World Bank's mandate. As the world community gathers in Copenhagen, the Bank stands ready to play its part in a framework of cooperative action—mobilizing resources, financing investments in physical and human capital, and supporting policy reforms, to advance social development.

Armeane M. Choksi
Vice President
Human Resources Development
and Operations Policy
The World Bank

Acknowledgments

THIS PAPER WAS WRITTEN BY EMMANUEL Y. ABLO IN COLLABoration with Barbara Bruns, Oey Astra Meesook, Jane Armitage, Indermit Gill, Jee-Peng Tan, and Carol Graham. The work was carried out under the overall guidance of K. Y. Amoako. The paper draws on extensive analytical work done both within and outside the Bank and was especially aided by the background papers written by Lionel Demery, Binayak Sen, Tara Vishwanath, Kalanidhi Subbarao, Jeanine Braithwaite, Jyotsna Jalan, and Michael Cernea. Extensive comments and suggestions were provided by World Bank staff in the regions and in the central vice presidencies, and in particular by the 1995 WDR team on labor and development. Representatives of several nongovernmental organizations also provided helpful comments. Bruce Ross-Larson was the principal editor. Margaret Igoe, Patricia Sanchez, and Josephine Carreon provided word processing assistance.

Executive Summary

DESPITE SUBSTANTIAL ECONOMIC AND SOCIAL PROGRESS IN the past few decades, there is still much human suffering. More than a billion people live in poverty, and rich countries as well as poor face high unemployment, which is especially acute in the formerly communist countries. Compounding the problems of poverty and unemployment is the threat of social disintegration, manifested in crime, violence, conflict, and war. Armed conflicts have led to the loss of more than 20 million lives since 1945, inflicted suffering on millions of others, and caused massive refugee and forced migration problems.

Globally, real per capita gross domestic product has risen by more than 3 percent a year since the mid-1960s. But only a handful of developing countries have sustained this—or higher—income growth over long periods. By contrast, progress on social indicators has been sustained. Despite uneven growth, infant mortality rates have been declining, and life expectancy and literacy rates rising, in all regions. Still, much remains to be done to improve the quality of life for large numbers of people, especially in Sub-Saharan Africa and South Asia.

Much remains to be done to improve the quality of life for large numbers of people.

The strategy that has proved effective in improving economic and social well-being, and the one discussed in the paper, consists of three elements: labor-demanding growth, investments in education and health, and safety nets for poor and vulnerable groups. Increasingly, a fourth element—good governance—is being added, because governments directly control a significant share of national resources and shape the policy environment for private economic agents and civil society. In the interest of economic and social progress, the use of public resources must emphasize efficiency and equity. Beyond that, the most important attributes of good governance are accountability, transparency, and participation. Participation, for example, increases stakeholders' ownership of policies and projects—which contributes to their willingness to share costs and maintain the assets created. Such involvement in turn raises the quality and sustainability of development programs and helps to build local capacity.

Social development requires a judicious mix of government and private involvement.

Governments can contribute to economic and social progress by focusing on the things that they do best. At one extreme are public goods—law and order, national security, and an environment conducive to business—which only a government can provide. At the other extreme are sectors in which private producers are active and efficient, but where selective government intervention is sometimes needed to correct market imperfections or failures. In other areas there is need for a judicious mix of government and private involvement—in health, education, physical infrastructure, agricultural research and extension, and protecting the weak and vulnerable members of society. What really matters is how effective and efficient a government is in discharging its responsibilities. And because administrative capacity is often weak in developing countries, governments need to choose the areas of intervention carefully and give priority to institution-building.

From Africa to Latin America, Asia, and the former communist countries, there is now a better appreciation of the role of the private sector in development and a greater readiness of all but a handful of countries to embark on market-oriented economic reforms. The core policies are prudent fiscal and monetary management, realistic exchange rates, open trade and investment regimes, and competitive markets in goods, capital, and labor. Also important is reorienting public spending toward basic social services (primary education, essential health services) that benefit the poor the most.

When implemented with commitment, policy reforms benefit the poor. But some reforms, particularly those involving cuts in the government budget deficit, can hurt the poor—and require safety nets. And to protect the political viability of reform programs, governments may also need to provide safety nets for some of the adversely affected who are not poor, such as workers laid off as a result of privatization or reductions in the size of the civil service.

Policy reform must cover labor market policies also. A well-functioning labor market can help ensure that growth is labor-demanding, that workers gain entry into jobs in which they can use their skills most productively, and that accurate signals are provided for investments in human capital. Carefully designed policies can also help insure households against lost income—and ease economic restructuring and reduce its social costs. And in setting basic labor standards, governments have to resist prematurely raising workplace standards and increasing job security for a few while reducing employment or driving employers into the informal sector.

Investments in human capital are crucial to economic and social progress.

Sound economic policies and a well-functioning labor market are essential for growth and employment generation, but they are not enough. Investments in human capital are equally crucial to economic and social progress. Human capital—knowledge, skills, and good health—is required for productive employment, informed and active citizenship, and a higher quality of life. Important links among human resource investments can and should be exploited to extract the most benefit from each dollar spent. Better nutrition, for example, helps children lead healthier lives and improves their capacity to learn—and their subsequent performance in the labor market. Basic education and health services with universal or wide coverage should have first call on limited public resources, and in education special attention should be given to girls' enrollment, as it usually lags behind that of boys. Governments also need to pay attention to the efficiency of resource use, for there are wide variations in the effectiveness of social spending across developing countries. In all this, they need to encourage and facilitate private involvement in the provision of education and health services.

Economic and social development is at the core of the World Bank's mandate—to help countries reduce poverty through sustainable growth and investments in people. Development must be people-oriented and include efforts to reduce inequality and better manage economic change. In this regard the Bank is increasingly emphasizing improved governance, which is essential for sound economic management and social stability. Within its mandate the Bank supports the efforts of borrowing members to improve public sector management, economic and financial accountability, legal systems, and transparency in the conduct of public affairs.

Development must be people-oriented and include efforts to reduce inequality and better manage economic change.

In recent years the Bank has dramatically increased its investments in people—from about 5 percent of total lending in the early 1980s to 15 percent in 1994. The composition of those investments also is changing, with more emphasis on primary education, girls' education, and primary health care. The Bank now lends more than $2 billion a year for education, $1 billion for health, and $200 million for population activities, making it the world's largest financier of investments in people. It is also the largest lender for AIDS prevention programs—with total lending now approaching $600 million.

Bank lending will continue to shift toward human resource development.

The Bank will continue to help governments implement policy reforms and assist with the provision of social safety nets to mitigate the transitional costs. To improve its development effectiveness, the Bank is emphasizing beneficiary participation in project selection, design, and implementation. It is also expanding its use of public expenditure reviews, poverty assessments, and social assessments as tools in the development of its country assistance strategies and in its dialogue with borrowers. Bank lending will continue to shift toward human resource development, with new commitments expected to reach $15 billion over the next three years. Lending to support improvements in public sector management and in the legal and regulatory framework, and thus in governance, also is expected to increase—in response to demands from borrowers. Finally, the Bank will strengthen strategic alliances with its partners in development, drawing on the comparative advantage of each organization. In particular, it will work:

- in partnership with countries and other agencies to mobilize greater external resources in support of economic and social development and to carry out the social development agenda agreed to at the Social Summit in Copenhagen.
- with governments and other agencies to support institutional development and capacity-building, including greater local involvement in the design, preparation, and supervision of Bank-supported projects and programs and in economic and social analysis.
- with other donors to encourage microenterprises and promote small-scale environmental initiatives.
- in collaboration with UN agencies and other donors to improve baseline information on poverty and to develop sustainable poverty monitoring systems to help governments assess progress in reducing poverty.

The goal of economic and social development is to improve the lives of people everywhere—reducing widespread poverty, spreading opportunities for more productive work, and pulling societies together for the equitable and participatory advancement of common purposes.

CHAPTER 1

Progress in Social Development

POVERTY HAS INCOME AND NONINCOME DIMENSIONS, which are usually intertwined. The poor have meager incomes; they are often illiterate and in poor health; they have a short life span. Although these conditions persist all over the world, living standards have been improving.

Income measures show some improvement: globally, real per capita GDP has increased by more than 3 percent a year since the mid-1960s. But among the developing countries only the East Asian miracle countries have been able to sustain this—or even higher—income growth for long periods. The income gap between the industrial countries and a large group of developing countries has thus widened.

Improvements in social indicators have been sustained across all regions for much of the past quarter century.

Improvements in social indicators, by contrast, have been sustained across all regions for much of the past quarter century. In health, for example, there have been improvements in life expectancy and infant mortality in all regions, even though per capita incomes stagnated or fell in some regions in the 1980s. Between 1965 and 1992 life expectancy in Sub-Saharan Africa increased from 43 to 52 years, and in South Asia from 47 to 60 years. Over the same period life expectancy rose from 53 to 68 years in East Asia and the Pacific, and in Latin America and the Caribbean from 58 to 68 years. The infant mortality rate also has fallen, though large regional differences remain. In 1992 it was 96 per thousand live births in Sub-Saharan Africa and 82 in South Asia, compared with 36 in East Asia and the Pacific.

Five factors could account for the continued improvement in health conditions, even in the face of declining per capita incomes. First, the earlier investments in health have continued to yield benefits. Second, the availability of low-cost health interventions has made it possible to reduce child mortality significantly. Third, the supply of medical services, financed from public resources and increasingly from private sources, has been greatly expanded. Fourth, the spread of education has increased awareness of the measures needed to prevent or combat disease. Fifth, expanded access to safe drinking water has reduced the incidence of waterborne diseases.

Besides the generally improving health conditions, there have been big gains in education. Primary school enrollment has expanded rapidly in all regions. In 1965 East Asia and the Pacific and Latin America and the Caribbean were only a small step from achieving universal primary school enrollment—and they moved quickly to do just that. In Sub-Saharan Africa, by contrast, the gross primary school enrollment rate, less than 50 percent in 1965, is now around 70 percent. As access to education has expanded, adult illiteracy rates have declined throughout the developing world, but Sub-Saharan Africa and South Asia lag behind, with adult illiteracy rates still more than 50 percent.

Remaining Challenges

About a third of the total population of developing countries survives on less than a dollar a day.

DESPITE THE PROGRESS IN IMPROVING LIVING STANDARDS over the past quarter century, reducing poverty remains a big challenge. More than one billion people—about a third of the total population of developing countries—are desperately poor, struggling to survive on less than a dollar a day. Hundreds of millions more have incomes barely above this threshold and thus face the constant risk of sinking below it. More than 130 million children of primary school age, most of them girls, are not attending school. And hundreds of millions of people still lack access to safe drinking water and proper sanitation, while three million or more people die each year from such diseases as tuberculosis and malaria.

With high population growth rates in the face of low or negative GDP growth rates, the number of people in poverty has risen in all regions except East Asia and the Pacific. On current trends this number will increase through at least the end of this century, even though some regions will see declines in the number of poor. In Sub-Saharan Africa, on the dollar-a-day measure, about 210 million people are in poverty, and their numbers continue to grow. In South Asia the share of the population in poverty has been declining, but the total number of poor is still very large—about 500 million people.

The challenges of poverty are not the same across all regions. In some regions, especially Sub-Saharan Africa and South Asia, economic and social progress means lifting people out of poverty. In the former Soviet Union and the countries of Eastern Europe, by contrast, the urgent task is to prevent previously middle-income countries from regressing into low-income countries, owing to the collapse of production systems and social services. Data are not available to measure the deterioration of social services, but there are indications that the problem is serious in many of the countries of the former Soviet Union and Eastern Europe—and that large numbers of people are slipping back into poverty.

The statistics on the poor make gloomy reading. But some countries with good policies, effective institutions, and strong commitment have shown that average incomes can be raised and social indicators improved dramatically—thus reducing poverty. Indonesia and Malaysia reduced the proportion of people in poverty by 60 percent or more in 10 to 20 years. Other countries—Botswana, the Republic of Korea, and Singapore—have been similarly successful in raising real per capita GDP and expanding access to social services. And the more recent success of Chile, China, and Mauritius shows that progress is possible once countries put in place policies and institutions conducive to faster growth and better living standards.

Some countries have raised average incomes and social indicators dramatically.

The prospects for developing countries also depend on the vicissitudes of the external economic environment. Today the world economy is characterized by favorable developments. World trade is buoyant and is likely to grow by 6 percent or more a year over the next 10 years. Globally, inflation is lower than it has been for a long time. International commodity prices have recovered from the depressed levels of the late 1980s and early 1990s. The conclusion of the Uruguay Round of trade talks represents further progress toward the opening of markets worldwide. The past few years have seen sharp increases in flows of both direct investment and portfolio investment to developing countries.

These are welcome developments for developing countries to capitalize on. But there also are problems and dangers. First, some low-income countries continue to be weighed down by a heavy burden of debt—signaling the need for further appropriate debt relief measures. Second, the bulk of the recent flows of private capital has gone to a few countries, mostly in East Asia and Latin America. Third, the climate in which con-

Sustained poverty reduction requires a combination of economic growth, investments in human capital, and safety nets for the poor.

cessional resources must be mobilized to support the development efforts of the low-income countries seems to be deteriorating. Fourth, the countries that depend heavily on commodity exports will continue to be vulnerable to sharp swings in world prices. The international development community can help to ease these constraints.

The Strategy for Poverty Reduction

COUNTRY EXPERIENCE SHOWS THAT SUSTAINED POVERTY reduction requires a combination of economic growth, investments in human capital, and safety nets for the poor. Economic growth is crucial—no country has achieved sustained improvements in living standards without it. And although sustaining growth is far from easy, there is ample evidence that the policy choices that countries make largely determine success or failure. From time to time countries must contend with forces beyond their control: droughts, floods, slumps in international commodity prices, and so on. Still, with sound economic management, they can deal better with these adverse forces.

Human capital, the product of education and improvements in health, also is critical to raising living standards. Because widespread literacy can launch a virtuous circle, universal primary education is key to developing human capital. By raising productivity, investments in education stimulate growth—and by opening up economic opportunities to more people, they contribute to reducing income inequality. Faster growth and less inequality in turn increase the supply of, and demand for, education. And a more educated labor force provides the basis for further improving productivity and sustaining growth.

To have impact on poverty, the benefits of economic growth must be widely shared.

To have the greatest impact on poverty, the benefits of economic growth must be widely shared. The more labor-demanding the growth, the more it improves living standards. Most countries that have had labor-demanding growth have also reduced income inequality, reinforcing increases in average incomes to boost living standards. Changes in inequality occur slowly. So, in all but a few cases marked rises in living standards have come about only when a country has sustained its economic growth.

How growth affects poverty depends greatly on the initial distribution of income. The more equal the distribution of income to start with, the more likely it is that poverty will be reduced for a given increase in average income. Indonesia and Zimbabwe provide an illustration of this point. In 1984 the proportion of the Indonesian population living in poverty was 39 percent, almost the same as Zimbabwe's 40 percent in 1991. With per capita GDP growth of 3.9 percent a year, Indonesia would have reduced the proportion of people in poverty to 24 percent by 1990 if income grew at the same rate for everybody. But for Zimbabwe to reduce its incidence of poverty to the same level with the same GDP growth rate, it would take longer—nine years rather than six.

Why? Because poverty is less sensitive to growth in Zimbabwe than in Indonesia. Many of Zimbabwe's poor have incomes far below the poverty line and so do not get out of poverty as readily as the poor in Indonesia when the economy grows. A further point: the way the growth process affects income inequality has an impact on how fast poverty is reduced. If growth results in less inequality, poverty reduction gets a further boost. This was the case in Indonesia, where the incidence of poverty came down to 22 percent in 1990. If growth had instead been associated with greater inequality, some of the opportunity for reducing poverty would have been lost. So, some of the advantages of the rapidly growing East Asian countries were their unusually low initial income inequality in 1960 and their labor-demanding pattern of growth, which tended to reduce income inequality over time.

As the foregoing discussion highlights, growth and human capital development usually improve living standards in the long run. But the strategy for raising living standards also requires a third element: safety nets for the poor and vulnerable. Safety nets take a variety of forms—such as cash transfers, targeted subsidies, public works schemes, and severance pay and retraining for laid-off public servants. With growth proving slow to resume in many reforming countries and with the former Soviet Union and the countries of Eastern Europe grappling with the difficult task of switching from socialist to market economies, the need for safety nets has come into sharper focus.

Good governance—the way governments exercise power and daily administrative responsibility in managing a country's human and economic resources—also must be part of the strategy for raising living standards. And accountability, transparency, and participation are among its most important attributes. Accountability means holding those in positions of authority responsible for their actions through the rule of law and due process rather than administrative fiat. Where accountability is

Good governance must be part of the strategy for raising living standards.

Participation raises the quality and sustainability of development programs.

lacking and corruption siphons off resources meant for development, the delivery of public services suffers—with detrimental effects on people's welfare, especially that of the poor. Greater transparency and accountability are mutually reinforcing, and without them the conduct of public policy tends to be plagued by alienation, suspicion, and social discontent. They need to be backed up by a legal and regulatory system that offers stability and predictability for business and civil society.

Public participation means giving citizens a voice in government decisions and activities—not only through voting and representation but also through direct involvement in shaping and implementing programs that affect their lives and well-being. For an intolerably large number of people the world is still a place of exclusion. Yet a growing body of evidence shows that broad participation can help bring more development to more people.

Decades of development experience point to the importance of participation in reducing poverty more effectively. Participation increases stakeholders' ownership of policies and projects—contributing to their willingness to share costs and maintain the assets created. Such involvement in turn raises the quality and sustainability of development programs and helps to build local capacity. It increases equity by involving the poor and other groups in planning and implementation. And it encourages transparency, accountability, and better institutional performance.

The potential benefits from increased participation are enormous. Realizing them, however, requires that governments establish institutional frameworks and decentralized processes that allow their people greater involvement in the decisions that affect their lives. Promoting market-oriented policies and private sector development goes some way toward achieving this goal, as it broadens participation in economic decisionmaking. And development institutions need to integrate participatory approaches into their operations by listening more closely to governments and other stakeholders.

CHAPTER 2

The Critical Role of Government

GOVERNMENTS CAN CONTRIBUTE MOST TO economic and social progress by focusing on the things that they do best. Sustained improvement in living standards through growth, human capital development, and safety nets requires a strong partnership between government and the private sector. Governments need to provide goods and services—law and order, national security, and an environment conducive to business and the smooth functioning of civil society—that only the state can provide. And even where activities fall in the domain of private economic agents, governments sometimes must correct market failures, but without creating vast and costly administrative and bureaucratic structures. There also are areas where neither the government nor the private sector can carry the entire responsibility. In such areas—health, education, infrastructure, and agricultural research and extension—a judicious blend of government and private effort is needed. Finally, for social reasons governments need to protect the weak and vulnerable members of society and provide safety nets for the poor.

Sustained improvement in living standards requires a strong partnership between government and the private sector.

The main or sole factor of production of the poor usually is their labor, which, except for low productivity, would earn them a decent living. Governments can best help the poor increase their productivity by investing in basic education. Although formal education does not by itself guarantee productivity increases, it opens up opportunities for the poor to share in the fruits of growth. One defining characteristic of the rapidly growing East Asian countries is that in 1960 they were well ahead of most countries at similar stages of development in schooling, educational attainment, and skilled labor. All except Indonesia had achieved—or were close to achieving—universal primary school enrollment. To help the poor develop their human capital fully, governments also need to invest in health, nutrition, and safe water supply.

In many developing countries the bulk of the labor force is in agriculture, where most households eke out a precarious existence. Governments need to invest in rural infrastructure and new agricultural technologies to raise productivity in this important sector. They also can help poor farmers increase their productivity by facilitating their access to land and credit. Where land ownership is highly concentrated—as in Mexico, the Philippines, South Africa, and Zimbabwe—land reform could promote equity and allow the poor to contribute more to economic growth. Korea used land reform to broaden support for government policies and to bolster political stability. Governments also need to pay attention to the credit requirements of the poor, because lack of access to credit often is the major constraint on the ability of poor farmers (and other small-scale entrepreneurs) to expand production. But access to schools, land, credit, and other assets is not enough. To ensure that the poor find work, governments need market-oriented policies to promote economic growth that is labor-demanding.

Inequality, another important concern for governments, often has different origins. In many countries it arises when indigenous, ethnic, racial, linguistic, and religious groups and women are kept in an inferior economic and social position. Disadvantaged groups invariably have less access to schooling and lower literacy rates. They tend to have worse health, nutrition, and other social indicators than the rest of the population. The lower education and poorer health status of women, minorities, and indigenous people reduce their incomes, through lower productivity and lower wages.

Equity issues take on added importance where the distribution of income is very unequal, as in many countries in Latin America, where the poorest 20 percent of the population receives only 4 percent of the income. Poverty is highly correlated with ethnicity in Bolivia, Guatemala, Mexico, and Peru. And where inequality is linked to discrimination, poverty tends to remain intractable for some segments of the population, no matter how robust or how labor-demanding a country's overall economic growth. To reduce poverty under these circumstances, a country requires both sound economic policies and specific social policies directed at existing inequities (box 1).

Where inequality is linked to discrimination, poverty reduction requires both sound economic policies and specific social policies.

Few dispute that governments have an important role to play in reducing poverty. And few fail to recognize that effective governments—with a strong capacity to formulate and implement coherent public

Box 1 Discrimination and Development

SOCIETIES CONSIST OF INDIVIDUALS WHO BELONG TO GROUPS with diverse characteristics in terms of ethnicity, race, gender, and religion. In most countries certain groups systematically do worse than others. For example, unstable employment and lower earnings are more common among the indigenous than the nonindigenous people of Guatemala, among blacks than whites in Brazil, among the members of scheduled castes and tribal groups than the upper castes in India, and among women than men in nearly all countries. To the extent that these differences originate in historical disadvantages manifested in unequal opportunities or discrimination, they can persist—with severe costs for individuals and the economy. Policies that correctly address such inequalities can enhance economic growth, reduce poverty, and increase welfare.

One policy direction is ensuring that social services are evenly distributed among the population. In South Africa, because of unequal distribution of spending, one-third of blacks are illiterate, and a high proportion have no access to safe water and proper sanitation. Another policy is to create a level playing field by outlawing discriminatory practices and affording equal opportunities to all groups. For example, certain privileges or exclusions may apply to some groups but not others, and the public sector may systematically recruit from certain groups but not others. In addition to having direct redistributive effects, equitable public spending and the removal of discriminatory practices have a significant positive effect on efficiency. Targeted public spending, such as that on education, and equal employment opportunities can reinforce the incentives for disadvantaged groups to invest in their human capital. The result of the increase in the overall educational attainment of the labor force will be a more productive economy and a more equitable society.

policies and projects—can make a real difference in improving living standards. Public spending in developing countries typically amounts to 20 to 30 percent of GDP, and the efficient management of these resources is critical to growth, to human capital formation, and to the welfare of the poor. That management in turn requires a cadre of professionals who can formulate and implement government policies, but they are in short supply in many developing countries, especially in Sub-Saharan Africa. This is part of the reason why public administration is often weak, as manifested in ineffective tax collection, poorly managed

Public spending in developing countries typically amounts to 20–30 percent of GDP and efficient management is critical.

Building institutional capacity needs to figure prominently in any strategy to reduce poverty.

public expenditure, abandoned public health measures, poor law enforcement, and haphazard justice. Because poorly functioning bureaucracies give conflicting signals to the private sector, they also damage long-term investment. Building institutional capacity thus needs to figure prominently in any strategy to reduce poverty.

Today's rolling back of government to give more power to the private sector and to civil society does not imply a minimal role for the state. It implies a different role: ensuring that governments focus on what they can do well while letting the private sector expand into activities that it can handle best. Reorienting government in turn implies a heavy responsibility to invest in the development of basic human capital, protect the poor, and promote social cohesion. It also implies a responsibility for creating an economic environment that promotes the development of the private sector through stable rules of the game and market-oriented policies.

CHAPTER 3

The Economic Fundamentals: The Importance of Markets

AS MORE AND MORE GOVERNMENTS COME TO recognize the importance of sound economic management, the core policies needed to spur labor-demanding economic growth are no longer so controversial.[1] Two sets of policies are touched on here. One emphasizes the importance of macroeconomic stability and price incentives. Another consists of structural policies directed at removing biases against agriculture, restructuring public expenditure, building effective financial systems, and breaking down barriers to informal sector activities.

Sustaining Macroeconomic Stability and Maintaining Price Incentives

PRICE INCENTIVES WORK BEST IN A STABLE ECONOMIC ENVIronment, and the key to macroeconomic stability is fiscal and monetary discipline.

- **Sustaining macroeconomic stability.** Most countries recognize that long-run sustainable growth requires low and stable inflation and a viable external payments position. This requires avoiding large deficits in the current account of the balance of

[1] *World Development Report 1991* discusses these in much greater detail.

payments and unsustainable government budget deficits and excessive money and credit expansion. Reducing the fiscal deficit often calls for actions on two fronts: eliminating wasteful expenditures and improving domestic revenue collection.

- **Maintaining a realistic exchange rate and open trade and investment regimes.** For a long time exchange rate policy was the most contentious of policies. That has changed. Most countries now realize that pricing foreign exchange correctly—without having to artificially suppress demand for it—is good for growth and good for equity. Opening economies to international trade and investment also is an effective way to promote growth. When international flows of goods, services, capital, labor, and technology have expanded quickly, the pace of economic advance has been rapid.
- **Allowing the price mechanism to work.** There is now a much wider recognition of the wisdom of having governments do things that they do best and relying on market forces to allocate most resources. Although not infallible, markets provide the most effective mechanism for mediating the desires and aspirations of billions of people—something that would stretch the administrative capacity of governments.

Removing Biases Against Agriculture

INCENTIVES IN AGRICULTURE HAVE BEEN GROSSLY DISTORTED through taxes, tariffs, subsidies, and overvalued currencies (box 2). Most countries are moving to correct price distortions in agriculture to promote a more labor-demanding pattern of production. But they need to do more, by helping the poor—particularly women—gain access to land, credit, and extension services and by providing such rural infrastructure as feeder roads and water. They also need to liberalize domestic and export marketing. In some developing countries land reform is crucial, to get more out of farming and to ease the problems of rapid rural-urban migration. The payoffs to all this can be great. A flourishing agricultural sector has powerful multiplier effects on employment in nonfarm rural activities, as rising incomes in agriculture stimulate demand for consumer goods and services and agricultural inputs.

A flourishing agricultural sector has powerful multiplier effects on employment.

Box 2 Plundering Agriculture

A RECENT WORLD BANK STUDY (SCHIFF AND VALDES 1992) MEASured the burden of price-distorting policies on farmers in 18 countries from 1960 to 1985. The main findings:

- Indirect taxes on agriculture (primarily from industrial protection and exchange rate overvaluation) amounted to 22 percent on average and direct agricultural taxes to 8 percent. Farmers' total tax burden was therefore 30 percent.
- Price-distorting policies depressed the internal terms of agricultural trade by an average of 40 percent. In most countries, moreover, these distortions increased with time.
- High taxation of agriculture was associated with low growth in agriculture and with low growth in employment and overall GDP.
- Substantial public investment in agriculture did not compensate for adverse price policies.

The study recommends that excess tax burdens on agriculture—both direct and indirect—be removed and notes that, in most countries, this would help the vast majority of the very poor.

Restructuring Public Expenditure

PUBLIC EXPENDITURES OFFER SIGNIFICANT OPPORTUNITIES for promoting growth and the equitable distribution of its fruits. Investments in basic social services—primary education, primary health care, safe drinking water, sanitation, nutrition, and family planning—yield high payoffs for individuals as well as for society. Investments in rural infrastructure and new agricultural technologies are essential for raising the productivity of farmers. But governments are not channeling enough resources to these areas. A major part of the reason is excessive military spending in all but a handful of countries. Consider Sub-Saharan Africa. Its spending rose from less than 1 percent of GNP in 1960 to more than 3 percent in 1990—this, in countries that could not provide adequate immunization coverage for children or universal primary education. Since the end of the cold war military spending has been on the decline in industrial countries. But in the developing countries efforts to reduce it have been more isolated and more tentative. To

Public expenditures offer significant opportunities for promoting growth and the equitable distribution of its fruits.

release significant resources for essential economic and social services, bolder efforts are clearly needed.

Progress in restructuring public expenditure more generally has been excruciatingly slow. Budgeting continues to be incremental and often ad hoc, with allocations influenced more by political calculations than by economic considerations. The demands of organized, vocal, visible groups—normally not the poor—are often met at the expense of more deserving groups, such as children without access to primary schools or in need of immunization. And because of tremendous institutional and political inertia, even programs and projects that have outlived their usefulness continue to receive funding.

Building Effective Financial Systems

FINANCIAL MARKETS AND INSTITUTIONS, ESSENTIAL FOR MOBILIZING resources for development, are weak and underdeveloped in many developing countries. This, together with macroeconomic instability, explains the low private savings in many developing countries. In some, the problem stems partly from the government's dominance of banking and its tendency to intervene in credit allocation decisions—often compounded by inadequate supervision of both public and private financial institutions. Many governments have already moved to free interest rates. The remaining challenge is institution-building—opening the sector to competition, reorganizing or privatizing ailing state banks, and strengthening the capacity of the central bank and other regulatory agencies to supervise the financial system.

Poor people are willing and able to pay for unsubsidized financial services.

Small borrowers in particular face obstacles in gaining access to credit, even in the smallest amounts. High transaction costs, high perceived risks of default, lack of collateral, and social resistance all deter formal financial institutions from lending to small entrepreneurs, many of them poor women. But the record in several countries shows that poor people are willing and able to pay for unsubsidized financial services from small-scale credit intermediaries that fit their needs (box 3). Small-scale credit programs in such countries as Bangladesh, Colombia, Indonesia, and Thailand extend loans to women and the poor. They have low default rates, based on financial incentives for prompt repay-

Box 3 Successful Small-Scale Credit Programs

CREDIT INSTITUTIONS CAN REACH SMALL-SCALE ENTREPRENEURS, as shown by the diverse experiences of Thailand's Bank of Agriculture and Agricultural Cooperatives, Bangladesh's Grameen Bank, Indonesia's BKK and BRI-Unit Desa, and Colombia's Accion International. These institutions charge positive real interest rates to protect their long-term viability as financial institutions. They have low default rates, based on financial incentives for prompt repayment and mutual guarantee arrangements that rely on group solidarity to encourage borrowers to honor their repayment obligations. They use peer groups or local village leadership to select and approve borrowers. They emphasize staff training and incentives. And within the limits of financial prudence, they respond flexibly to the needs of borrowers—for example, by accepting nontraditional forms of collateral for loans. Although loans from these institutions at times appear expensive relative to commercial bank credit, they generally are substantially cheaper than funds from informal moneylenders, often the only other source available to poor people.

ment and mutual guarantee arrangements that encourage borrowers to honor their repayment obligations.

Removing Barriers to Informal Sector Activities

THE INFORMAL SECTOR, OPERATING WITH LITTLE SECURITY and capital, makes up 40 to 60 percent of the urban labor force in developing countries. High payroll taxes, investment licensing, business regulations, and other labor market regulations inhibit formal employment, pushing workers into informal activities. This is inefficient, because it transfers labor from high- to low-productivity activities. So, removing burdensome regulations can improve the allocation of labor to higher-productivity activities—and increase the labor intensity of production in the formal sector. Furthermore, poor workers in family-based firms or micro-enterprises often lack access to such basics as water and power. Targeting infrastructure investments to the poor can significantly increase their productivity and earnings.

Targeting infrastructure investments to the poor can significantly increase their productivity and earnings.

The burden of regulatory costs on the informal sector can be significant. A recent study in Argentina found that, despite the widespread assumption that informal businesses and micro-enterprises evade regulations, regulatory costs account for as much as 21 percent of their yearly expenditures. In some sectors, such as manufacturing and construction, regulatory costs can be as high as 44 percent of total costs. Micro-entrepreneurs may devise strategies to avoid costly regulations, but the evasive strategies themselves often entail high costs and forgone opportunities. During the start-up phase of a microfirm, state and local regulations impose the heaviest burden. During operations the highest regulatory costs come from national labor taxes (especially social security payments). These costs are powerful disincentives for microfirms to hire workers, so most rely heavily on the unpaid labor of family members.

CHAPTER 4

Policy Reforms, the Poor, and Safety Nets

THAT POLICY REFORMS NOT ONLY CONTRIBUTE TO economic growth but also work to the advantage of the poor can be illustrated in several ways. Take stabilization. Its aim is to move away from the imprudent fiscal and monetary polices that lead to rampant inflation. High and rising inflation hurts most economic agents, but because it is a regressive tax, it hurts the poor and those on fixed incomes more. The high inflation in many Latin American countries, notably in Brazil and Peru in the late 1980s and early 1990s, has contributed significantly to a worsening distribution of income and social disintegration. High inflation also hurts low-paid wage workers and farmers who produce crops subject to government price controls.

Policy reforms that contribute to growth work to the advantage of the poor.

In Uganda a combination of rising inflation and controlled producer prices discouraged the production of coffee, a smallholder crop. For the past three years inflation has been contained to a range of 5 to 10 percent—a sign of successful stabilization. This provides some relief to workers on meager wages. Together with an upturn in world coffee prices, it also is contributing to the recovery of coffee production.

But policies do not work in isolation. Uganda's liberalization of the agricultural sector—removing producer price controls, eliminating state marketing monopoly systems, and abolishing or lowering export taxes—has been another important factor behind the recent increases in the production of coffee and other crops. Until private traders were allowed into export marketing, Uganda's coffee, tea, and cotton farmers did not receive prompt payment for their crops—and sometimes were not paid at all. Now traders compete for their crops and pay them promptly.

Moving to a realistic exchange rate is another essential piece of policy reform that benefits the poor. An overvalued currency keeps the prices of imports artificially low. The people who benefit most from this policy are those who have access to foreign exchange and those who consume significant amounts of imported goods and services—not the poor. Very often, overvalued currencies are maintained at the expense of producers of export crops and other exports. In the franc zone countries of West Africa the profitability of such export crops as cocoa, coffee, and groundnuts—on which large numbers of the rural poor depend—was badly hurt by the prolonged overvaluation of the CFA franc, finally devalued in January 1994.

Removing barriers to informal sector activities is another reform beneficial to the poor. After agriculture, the informal sector is the most important source of employment in many developing countries. Yet most governments actively repress informal sector activities, mainly through licensing requirements and price controls. Where controls have been lifted—as in India, Peru, Tanzania, and Uganda—a vibrant private sector has emerged, absorbing new entrants to the labor force and many of those laid off during public sector downsizings. In Poland and Russia private sector growth has come mainly from new enterprises and businesses spun off formerly state-owned enterprises.

In the long term the reform of public spending promises even greater benefits for the poor. The objectives of reform are:

- To increase social spending while maintaining fiscal prudence.
- To redirect the increased social spending toward services that benefit the poor, especially basic education and essential health services.
- To increase allocations for feeder roads, agricultural research and extension, and rural and peri-urban water supply.

In many countries restructuring public expending in this way means reducing military expenditure, withdrawing subsidies to state enterprises, and stopping prestige projects—hard choices, but necessary to control the deficit and keep inflation low. Encouragingly, some countries are moving in this direction. In Uganda over the past two years, the government has reduced the size of its military forces by almost half. It also has embarked on a process of both protecting and increasing spending on primary education, basic health services, feeder roads, agricultural research and extension, and the police and the judiciary.

The reform of public spending promises greater benefits for the poor.

Safety Nets

SOME REFORMS, PARTICULARLY THOSE ASSOCIATED WITH DEFICIT reduction or monetary contraction, can hurt the poor. But what hurts the poor most is prolonged economic decline of the kind that has beset most countries of Sub-Saharan Africa. Because sustaining the old policies would mean continuing declines in living standards, policy reforms have become inevitable. And because governments have to be attentive to the adverse effects on the poor and some others who lose out (laid-off civil servants, for example), reforms should incorporate safety nets for the poor. In choosing the instruments of social protection—and their duration and coverage—governments must confront many key issues, including financing, targeting, and the choice of delivery mechanisms.

In designing safety nets, governments confront issues of financing, targeting, and the choice of delivery mechanisms.

Financing. Since resources are limited, there are tradeoffs between long-term investment in growth and human resources and short-term investments in safety nets. Excessive spending on safety nets can deplete the investible resources for growth, and inadequate spending can accentuate poverty in the short run and impair reforms in the medium run. Such tradeoffs are starker in the countries of the former Soviet Union than elsewhere, given the large declines in output since 1990. In both adjusting and transitional economies any safety net program that imposes a heavy fiscal drain has no chance of being sustained.

Targeting. Governments implementing difficult policy reforms often have to contest strong, organized opposition and assuage vocal, less needy groups with some compensation. But reforms can also provide governments with opportunities to redirect resources to the poor—say, by revamping untargeted programs—and have a salutary impact on the budget (box 4). Even where administrative capacity is weak, geographic location or the quality of the subsidized good can be used to target the needy.

Choice of delivery mechanisms. There are two problems with assistance delivered from the top (governmental agencies) to the beneficiaries in villages. First, the beneficiaries often are not correctly identified, so that benefits leak to the nonpoor. Second, even if the beneficiaries are identified, the benefits often do not conform to their needs. To identify the poor correctly and deliver assistance cost-effectively, some countries (Bolivia, Egypt) have experimented with social funds, allowing communities to determine their own social investment priorities and to help

Box 4 Jordan Revamps Food Subsidies to Cut Costs

BEFORE JORDAN'S ECONOMIC REFORM, OPEN-ENDED FOOD subsidies cost 3.2 percent of GDP and were the single largest item contributing to the fiscal deficit. With reform, general subsidies on bread and barley—the food staples of the poor—were retained, but prices were increased to cover part of the transfer. General subsidies on rice, sugar, and milk, however, were replaced by a system of quantity-specific food coupons that took into account the size of the household. Subsidy costs fell dramatically—from 3.2 to 1.4 percent of GDP. Some 25,000 families identified as below the poverty line received direct income support through a new cash transfer. By changing in-kind benefits and introducing a new cash benefit, Jordan managed to cushion particularly vulnerable groups from the short-run pain of adjustment while bringing overall spending down to sustainable levels.

implement and maintain the assets created. Others (many countries in Europe and Central Asia, India) have used decentralized administrative units, such as local authorities. And still others (Bolivia, Benin, El Salvador) have used nongovernmental agencies as alternatives to delivery by government agencies.

The success of safety net programs depends on whether they are depoliticized, decentralized, and rooted in strong community-based initiatives and organizations. Consider social funds. Demand-driven, they clearly are a departure from other programs. The social fund in Bolivia enlisted NGO participation and reached the poor, and the one in Peru is encouraging grassroots involvement and attracting strong political commitment. The central feature behind the success of Mexico's PRONASOL—an umbrella program to deliver health, nutrition, education, housing, and infrastructure to the poor—is beneficiary participation. And El Salvador's Fund for Social Investment, created in 1990, has an impressive record of working with NGOs in targeting assistance to the poor.

Safety nets should be an integral part of economic reforms.

Safety nets should be an integral part of the overall package of economic reforms, not added on after the reform has been initiated. In Sri Lanka the program of economic restructuring was accompanied by a safety net targeted to the poor (box 5). Unless the outreach of programs and benefits is held in check—and targeting is effective—adverse effects on incentives to work are inevitable. Until the end of the 1970s every

Box 5 Sri Lanka Integrates Safety Nets with Economic Reforms

SRI LANKA HAS A LONG HISTORY OF SUBSTANTIAL PUBLIC INvestment in health and education. As part of the 1989 economic reforms, the Janasaviya Program provided poor people with fixed, monthly cash grants for two years to acquire skills to become microentrepreneurs. Of these monthly grants, 60 percent was released to households. The balance—the "savings" component—was made available to them at the end of the two-year period to start an enterprise. In return for the monthly cash payments during the two years, beneficiary households were required to provide 20 days of labor every month, either for their own training or for community work on infrastructure projects. The program is being introduced throughout Sri Lanka in successive, geographically defined rounds, with the poorest areas covered first.

citizen of Sri Lanka had access to subsidized rice. But as the program became fiscally unsustainable, the government moved in early 1980 to a food stamp program—and targeted it to households below the poverty line, using self-declared incomes as a means test. Even in 1991 the number of beneficiary households was twice as high as the number under the poverty line. Loose targeting of the food stamp program is estimated to have reduced the work effort (labor supply) of participants by three to five days a month. By contrast, food stamps targeted to pregnant and lactating women and to children under five registered at the primary health care centers in Jamaica have restricted the scope of the program to the neediest.

Self-targeted safety net programs generally lead to better outcomes and are more effective in reaching the poor than programs with income-based means tests. Public works in Bangladesh, Chile, and India have had a major impact on the poor, essentially because of self-targeting. Moreover, low wages in India and payment of wages in-kind in Zambia attracted women to the work sites. But India's massive nationwide credit-based asset (and income) generation program—the Integrated Rural Development Program—relied exclusively on income-based means tests for selecting beneficiaries. The outcome: a large share of benefits went to the nonpoor.

Self-targeted safety net programs generally are most effective in reaching the poor.

Gender-specific targeting of women may be necessary in safety net programs.

Gender-specific targeting of women may be necessary in safety net programs. Economic reforms, by their nature, are meant to make economies function more efficiently. Thus both men and women are expected to gain from such reforms in the long run. But the short-term benefits of reforms may be immediate for some women, but slow in reaching, or even absent for, others. Hence, the need in some instances to target safety nets to women.

To promote essential economic reforms and to gain political support or consensus, it may be necessary to put in place programs not only for the poor, but also for those directly affected by policy and institutional reforms, whether poor or not. To ease the implementation of public sector reforms, Argentina, the Gambia, and India have used one-time compensation to laid-off workers (such as railway workers and civil servants). Some Eastern European countries are resorting to severance pay and retraining as safety nets for workers in the formal sectors.

Safety net programs, however efficient and well targeted, are only temporary solutions. They cannot be effective in raising living standards on a sustained basis unless they are part of a broader process of economic reform that protects social spending during the reform period—and redirects it to the poor. For example, a drop in spending on health and education occurred in some of India's poorest states, which already spent the least on primary health care and primary education. Governments clearly need to combine safety net programs with a pro-poor redirection of social sector spending.

Safety net measures and social funds have become necessary instruments to contain and balance the adverse socioeconomic effects of policy reforms. The key lesson is that appropriately designed safety nets should be introduced alongside reforms, not after the reform program is under way.

Policy Reforms: Lessons of Experience

THE SORTS OF POLICY REFORMS DISCUSSED IN THIS PAPER have been under way for some time now in diverse countries, whose experiences provide valuable lessons for reform:

Good economic management helps immensely in avoiding problems—and in solving them. The severity of a country's economic distortions matters. Countries that suffered the worst declines in GDP during the 1980s were among the most heavily indebted—and had large terms of trade losses. These countries required radical debt relief, which was either slow in coming or inadequate when it came. But debt relief was not enough. They also had to make far-reaching policy changes, which many failed to do.

Broadly-based political consensus increases the chance of success. Building an understanding of the need for change and a sense of ownership of policy reforms—through consultation and dialogue with employers, trade unions, civic groups, professional associations, and other nongovernmental organizations—increased the likelihood of smooth and timely implementation of reforms.

Delay invites more painful reforms later. Countries that delayed reforms achieved lower growth and saw poverty worsen. When they finally decided to reform, they had to undertake wide-ranging programs, for which many lacked the capacity. Moreover, by delaying reforms, they allowed opposition to coalesce.

Comprehensive reform programs—to restore macroeconomic stability and microeconomic incentives and build institutional capacity—stand a better chance of reigniting growth and improving the conditions of the poor. Countries that adopted piecemeal measures or implemented reforms intermittently have generally failed to reap significant rewards. Until business confidence is restored in the government's economic management, the response to policy reform is bound to be muted.

Comprehensive reform programs stand a better chance of reigniting growth and improving the conditions of the poor.

Success depends largely on a country's own efforts. Increased external resource flows have been valuable in building physical and human capital and easing the pain of adjustment but have not guaranteed success. What has counted most is a country's commitment to reform.

Social spending on basic services should be protected. The level of public expenditure on the social sectors has usually been maintained during periods of policy reform. But by not paying attention to the composition of that spending, countries have often failed to shift resources to the basic services that benefit the poor the most.

Safety nets should be integrated into programs of policy reform. Protecting the poor and vulnerable during periods of economic reform is important for reducing poverty as well as for sustaining the reforms.

CHAPTER 5

Labor Market Policies

BEYOND THE ECONOMIC POLICIES DISCUSSED IN THE foregoing, policies that promote a well-functioning labor market can help ensure that growth is labor-demanding, that workers gain entry into jobs where they can use their skills most productively, and that accurate signals are provided for investments in human capital. Carefully designed policies also can help insure households against lost income—and ease economic restructuring and reduce its social costs. Conversely, inappropriate labor market regulations and interventions—especially those that reduce labor mobility or prematurely raise labor costs while protecting workers in the modern sector—can inhibit growth and job creation.

The most powerful way to improve labor market outcomes is through labor-demanding growth.

The most powerful way to improve labor market outcomes—employment, wages, workplace standards, and income security—is through labor-demanding growth that raises incomes and makes more and better jobs available to poor people. Governments should, of course, set basic labor standards. The freedom to organize and bargain collectively, the elimination of forced labor, the ending of discrimination at work, and the progressive elimination of child labor are objectives that should be supported everywhere. But premature attempts to raise workplace standards and increase job security can end up helping only a few while driving private employers to evade the regulations or move into the informal sector. Employment practices in the public sector that are out of line with the rest of the economy inevitably depress growth in the long run and rarely help the poorest workers. In any event, in most developing countries enforcing labor legislation outside the formal wage sector is difficult, if not impossible.

The main focus of labor policies should be to:

- Facilitate labor mobility by improving labor market information systems and increasing workers' skills.
- Reform labor legislation to remove excessive regulation that reduces employment, while improving the design of interventions intended to protect the poor and other vulnerable groups.
- Reduce overstaffing while promoting competitive pay in the public sector.

Facilitating Labor Mobility

Governments need to facilitate labor mobility by providing labor market information and encouraging training.

IN TODAY'S COMPETITIVE GLOBAL ENVIRONMENT—WITH FREquent job creation and destruction in response to changes in comparative advantage and patterns of demand—governments need to facilitate labor mobility. They can do this by providing labor market information to smooth job changes and by encouraging training to reduce skill mismatches.

Employment agencies often are the main vehicles for collecting and disseminating job-related information. Government agencies, needed to provide some targeted services, can coexist with private agencies. These should help poor people who may be unable to afford fees, young job-seekers who need career counseling, and experienced workers who have been displaced during mass restructuring. For example, Chile has agencies that target assistance to underskilled youth, using enterprise-based and privately provided training programs. But the usefulness of employment agencies is likely to be limited in countries where most employment opportunities are in small-scale, informal trade and service businesses.

Most worker training occurs on the job. But governments can encourage technical and vocational training to ease the school-to-work transition and to help dislocated and disadvantaged workers find appropriate work. Training in specific skills can be effective when it builds on a good general education, which increases workers' trainability and their adaptability to change. Public expenditures on training are most effective when combined with private provision. In Chile about two-thirds of the graduates of CODESSER schools—which have prominent employers on their boards—found employment soon after graduation. In Egypt, by contrast, graduates of vocational and technical schools being run by the government without employer participation joined the ranks of the unemployed. But this situation is changing, with many public and private sector firms focusing more on on-the-job training. At any rate, vocational training schemes do not create jobs on their own, and they are successful only if skilled jobs are available, which is most likely if modern wage employment is expanding. This raises questions about large public investments in retraining where, as in most of the formerly communist countries, the growth of the formal sector is sluggish.

Special labor market problems arise in countries undergoing a massive transition from one economic system to another. The extensive redeployment of labor imposes heavy social costs on the affected workers and their families. But workers can be helped in finding new jobs (box 6). Essential in this is balancing the level of protection with fiscal considerations and incentive effects on workers. In the long run the solution is rapid growth in private sector employment.

Reforming Labor Legislation

DECENT WORKING CONDITIONS AND SECURITY AGAINST the loss of income are desirable objectives everywhere. But it is essential that policies and programs minimize the adverse effects on labor market incentives. In developing countries with abundant unskilled labor there is a tradeoff between increasing standards and security and keeping labor costs low to favor a labor-demanding mix of output and technology. Favoring seemingly good jobs by encouraging higher benefits and job security for small groups of workers helps the insiders but can reduce employment growth in the formal sector, keeping outsiders—usually the poor—in low-productivity jobs in the unregulated sector.

Work conditions. Occupational health and safety legislation protects workers from such occupational and environmental hazards as exposure to toxic chemicals, and protection is especially necessary for such vulnerable groups as pregnant women, the uneducated, and workers with no bargaining power. Industrial tragedies—such as the one in Thailand in 1993 in which 102 workers, most of them women, died while locked in a toy factory that caught fire—underscore the need for minimum safety standards in all countries.

Encouraging higher benefits and job security for workers in the formal sector can hurt those—usually the poor—in the unregulated sector.

Box 6 Casualties of Change: Helping Labor in Transitional Economies

TRANSITIONAL ECONOMIES TODAY HAVE UNprecedented labor market problems. Severe declines in output, economic restructuring, and mass layoffs associated with privatization have increased unemployment and cut real wages. In single-industry towns layoffs to shed excess labor are particularly painful. The sharp fall in output also has led to an acute fiscal crisis. As demand for assistance to the unemployed and other hard-hit groups has increased, public resources to meet that demand have shrunk. Where growth in private sector employment is slow, governments need to step in to protect households from undue hardship, maintain investments in human capital, and ensure the political sustainability of economic reforms.

Labor market policies can make reform easier on labor and reduce its social cost. Passive measures—such as pensions and unemployment benefits—give unemployed and older workers some income security. Active measures—such as public works, microenterprise schemes, wage subsidies, training, job counseling, and information services—can help workers find new employment and reduce the need for spending on passive measures. But such measures cannot in themselves increase employment. To be cost-effective, these schemes must be temporary, well targeted, and designed to minimize disincentives to work.

Public works schemes, a promising alternative to passive schemes, have proved effective in countries as diverse as Chile and India. Experience shows that such schemes should pay below-market wages to avoid taking employees away from the private sector and remain financially sustainable. Public works programs are now being used to combat growing unemployment and rehabilitate basic social infrastructure Central and Eastern Europe.

Somewhat less promising are microenterprise schemes, training, and public employment agencies. Experience from OECD countries suggests that microenterprise schemes that promote self-employment have only limited potential for success. Even well-designed programs have attracted, at most, only 5 percent of the unemployed. Training to help workers acquire new skills also may look appealing, but it is expensive and unlikely to yield high returns in a stagnant or declining economy. Recent evidence from Hungary and Poland suggests that those finding jobs do so without first becoming unemployed, and those already unemployed are bypassed by privatized firms. If this trend is widespread, it would considerably limit the ability of employment agencies to assist the unemployed.

Job security. Governments need to find a balance between protecting workers from arbitrary dismissal and allowing employers to adjust to changing market conditions by laying off redundant or mismatched workers. Under current law in many countries dismissals for economic reasons are considered unjust: the process of firing or laying off workers is cumbersome, often making it difficult for businesses to stay profitable. This may discourage employers from hiring in the first place, hurting job growth. Brazil and Peru have tried to address this problem by setting up a severance fund financed by employer contributions, with benefits payable on severance, regardless of cause. In Chile all employer-initiated dismissals require that the employee receive a minimum severance payment. As in other countries, the employee has a right to sue the employer, but Chile has a set of transparent rules to determine whether the termination was unjust, in which case the employer must pay additional severance benefits.

Social insurance. Both industrial and developing countries use unemployment insurance as an alternative to severance pay to provide a safety net for workers during job changes. Unemployment insurance schemes also can facilitate better worker-firm matches. But they can distort employer and employee behavior—increasing the average length of unemployment, making employers more likely to lay off workers temporarily, and amplifying the fluctuations in employment. Distortions can be reduced if insurance schemes are financed not through general government funds but through employer contributions that are experience-rated. In the United States the more frequently employers lay off workers, the higher the premiums they pay. Disincentives for unemployed workers to look for a job can be minimized by limiting the level and duration of benefits and narrowly defining eligibility criteria. In the Czech Republic tightening eligibility and reducing the size and duration of unemployment benefits in 1992 held down unemployment rates and increased wage employment.

In many middle-income countries payroll taxes finance pension and health care insurance programs. High rates of payroll taxation—62 percent of wages in Hungary and 43 percent in Brazil—can discourage employment. Either they are borne by firms, pushing up labor costs and reducing labor demand as international competitiveness is eroded and firms switch to more capital-intensive technologies, or they result in lower wages for workers. And the desire to evade these regulations drives firms and labor into the informal sector, where poor access to credit and other inputs reduces productivity.

Better design of social insurance systems can reduce these adverse impacts on employment. In general, systems should mandate modest benefits to keep taxes low. And clear links between contributions and benefits help workers see contributions as part of their compensation package rather than as a tax. Chile, Malaysia, and Singapore have successfully used employer and employee taxes to fund individual retirement schemes. Employer-run pension plans, common in many countries, can limit labor mobility, as workers lose previously accumulated

Better design of social insurance systems can reduce adverse impacts on employment.

pensions when they move from one job to another. Establishing a national pension system or laws that guarantee pension portability removes this disincentive.

Protecting vulnerable groups. While flexible labor markets are essential for economic growth, the simple equation of more flexibility with less government intervention is flawed. Governments have a moral responsibility to shield workers whose bargaining power is weak. Legislation often is insufficient and may need to be supplemented by direct interventions on behalf of these groups. Minimum wage laws, unemployment insurance, severance payments, and job security legislation cannot be used to help the rural and informal sector workers who form the bulk of the poor in developing countries. But job programs financed from general revenues, such as India's Employment Guarantee Scheme and Chile's public works programs, can help provide income security for poor households. Senegal's AGETIP, a private nonprofit agency set up to implement the government's infrastructure investments, has also assisted in creating a market for unskilled labor and encouraging small entrepreneurs.

Legislation addressing the special circumstances of women can be designed so that it does not unduly raise the costs of employing women relative to men.

Women in the labor market. Legislation addressing the special circumstances of women can be designed so that it does not unduly raise the costs of employing women relative to men. Maternity leave and benefits alleviate some of the physical and financial demands on pregnant women and new mothers, but when these benefits are financed by employers, they increase women's labor costs and can lead to discrimination in hiring or to lower wages for women. Having all employees and employers contribute to a social insurance fund that provides support for pregnant and nursing mothers during absences from work is a promising alternative.

Some apparently gender-neutral laws can have gender-biased outcomes. Restrictions on the length of time a worker can be hired under a temporary contract—intended to give teeth to legislation regarding nonwage benefits and job security for permanent workers—may inadvertently hurt women. Because women move in and out of the labor force and change sectors more often than men, these restrictions may lead employers to prefer hiring males.

Legislation to protect women workers should thus take into account both the beneficial and the adverse effects. Where effective, legislation is likely to help women in the protected sector where the better-off workers are to be found. Government also can do more in providing low-wage employment for poor women. Public works programs in Africa, designed well, have increased women's participation in work (box 7).

Child labor. Child labor, one of the most appalling manifestations of poverty, is pervasive in many parts of the world, especially in agriculture. It usually contributes to reducing the poverty of households, but at the cost of the children's education and future well-being. Income uncertainty, household size, and schooling opportunities are key determinants of the supply of child labor. Because children from larger households are less likely to attend school and more likely to work at home, women's education, improvements in women's health, and population programs can help reduce child labor by helping to reduce family size. Financial incentives—such as stipends to compensate families for the loss of their children's labor—may be necessary to persuade them to send their children to school.

Women's education, improvements in women's health, and population programs can help reduce child labor.

Promoting equitable economic growth, reducing poverty and income risk, increasing school attendance (particularly by girls) and reducing

Box 7 Women's Participation in Public Works

RECENT PUBLIC WORKS PROGRAMS IN BURKINA FASO, BURUNDI, Rwanda, Sudan, Tanzania, and Zambia suggest that obstacles to women's employment outside the home can be removed. Even such programs as road improvement, irrigation development, and other construction projects not typically regarded as women's work have attracted work forces that were as much as 60 percent female.

Recognizing that women are less likely than men to visit job sites or administrative centers, these projects launched massive publicity programs through the media to inform them that work was available in public projects. When public meetings were held, women were given enough lead time to reschedule their household activities and obtain permission from spouses or parents. Public works programs were particularly successful in recruiting women when jobs involved work similar to that performed by women at home or on the farm. In afforestation projects in Rwanda and the Sudan, for example, women were hired to tend tree nurseries. It also helps to adjust the form and frequency of compensation to women's preferences. In Niger women preferred to be paid with food, or a combination of food and cash, at the end of each day, because this allowed them to address the family's survival needs immediately.

desired fertility—all these are likely to reduce child labor to levels that legislation can address. Laws on child labor should be tailored to the institutional and administrative capacity of a country and directed to extreme forms of child labor, such as child prostitution, bonded labor, and work in hazardous conditions.

Reforming Public Sector Employment and Pay

BECAUSE OF OVERSTAFFING, A PERVASIVE IRONY AFFLICTS public sector employment in many developing countries: the overall salary bill is too high even while wage rates are too low. Faced with a need for fiscal cutbacks, governments maintain or even expand employment but allow real wages to fall. Overstaffing in the public sector burdens government budgets and can siphon off much-needed resources for education and health. Poor pay policies also can give rise to rent-seeking, moonlighting, and corruption by public officials—lowering their productivity and that of entrepreneurs. Another problem of public pay is wage compression across skill categories, making it difficult for governments to attract talented administrators.

The best way to reduce the government wage bill is to restrict the growth of public employment.

The best way to reduce the government wage bill is to restrict the growth of public employment. Governments generally should not be involved in commercial activities. Where privatization leads to mass layoffs, governments need to ease the transition to new employment—say, through temporary public works programs or compensation packages. In Chile after the privatization of 200 of 260 public enterprises in 1974 and in response to an economic recession, the government stepped in with public works programs. In just one year employment in these schemes grew from zero to more than 15 percent of total public employment. Scaled-down versions of these programs were in place for more than 10 years until a sustained economic recovery finally set in. In Argentina a substantial compensation package for affected workers facilitated the privatization of the railways.

Sound economic policies and a well-functioning labor market are essential for growth and employment generation. But so are investments in human capital, which can have far-reaching benefits for the individual and society.

CHAPTER 6

Developing Human Capital

ECONOMIC STABILITY, THE RIGHT INCENTIVE STRUCTURE, an open economy, well-functioning labor markets, and access to world markets all provide the necessary cornerstone for successful economic and social development. But countries also need human capital to develop. There is not a choice between human capital and sound economic policies—it must be both. In the 1960s and 1970s many countries ignored the policy environment while making large investments in physical capital. The rates of return on these investments were generally low and even negative. Just as with physical capital, investments in people will not be productive unless the policy and institutional context in which investment takes place is conducive to development. As Gary Becker, a Nobel Laureate in Economics, put it recently, "If you invest only in human capital, you are not going to be able to succeed if you have a bad economic system. If you have a good system and you neglect human capital, you are also not going to do so well. But if you do both, it is going to be more productive than either component alone."

Investing in people's education, health, nutrition, and family planning is one of the keys to economic growth and social progress.

Investing in people's education, health, nutrition, and family planning is one of the keys to economic growth and social progress. It creates knowledge, broadens skills, and improves health—the human capital so essential for sustaining economic growth, raising living standards, and enriching people's lives. And because the poor have few assets, investing in their human capital often is the best way to equip them to become more productive. Beyond the gains to individuals, such investments also benefit society. Widespread literacy, for example, strengthens the institutions of civil society and of governance.

Human Capital for Higher Living Standards

INVESTMENTS IN EDUCATION, PARTICULARLY IN PRIMARY EDUCAtion, boost economic growth. A recent World Bank study, *The East Asian Miracle: Economic Growth and Public Policy*, shows that the single most important factor in launching the miracle countries on a path of rapid, sustained economic growth was universal or near-universal primary school enrollment. Universal primary schooling gave these countries a crucial advantage over other countries. In 1960 Pakistan and Korea had similar levels of income, but by 1985 Korea's GDP per capita was nearly three times Pakistan's. This outcome is explained largely by the difference in initial primary school enrollment rates between the two countries. In 1960 fewer than a third of the children of primary school age were enrolled in Pakistan while nearly all were enrolled in Korea.

The benefits of education show up clearly for individuals. Education expands the capacity of people to make better use of technology and inputs, exploit new information, and adapt more effectively to change. For men in Côte d'Ivoire an extra year of schooling enhanced earnings by 12 percent, after controlling for other factors. In Ghana, Malaysia, and Peru an extra year of schooling boosted farmers' output by 2 to 5 percent, after controlling for farm size, inputs, and hours worked. In Thailand farmers with four years of schooling were three times as likely to adopt new fertilizers and other modern inputs as farmers with one to three years of schooling.

Education has a powerful impact on women's productivity. In agriculture the returns to an additional year of women's education can range as high as 15 percent where modern technology has been introduced—about the same as the returns for men. Educated women also are more productive in their role as caregivers in the home. Demographic and health surveys in 25 developing countries have shown that child mortality is about 15 percent lower when the mother has had one to three years of schooling.

Education has a powerful impact on women's productivity.

The contribution of a mother's education to lower fertility, child mortality, and maternal mortality are such that an extra year of primary schooling for a thousand women in India would cost $32,000 but yield a social benefit of $52,000 (after allowing for the lag between when girls are educated and when they grow up and become mothers). Similarly, in Kenya and Pakistan the social benefits of educating girls are big enough to cover the costs of the investment, even before including the benefits of maternal education for adult health (including that of husbands and other adult relatives) and market activities.

Better health and nutrition produce benefits in the next generation as well.

Improving people's nutrition and health also can bring substantial economic and social benefits. Healthier and better nourished people lose fewer days of work, are more productive on the job, and enjoy longer working lives. Better health also makes it possible for people to organize economic activities more productively.

Better health and nutrition produce benefits in the next generation as well—through their effects on children's physical and intellectual development, which affects their subsequent productivity as adults. A child's early home environment is key: malnutrition, poor sanitation, limited access to health care, and lack of intellectual stimulation all work to reduce a child's potential later in life. In China and Thailand children lagging behind in height-for-age, a sign of chronic malnutrition, typically fall behind the grade normally attained by children of the same age. Studies suggest that a child's height by age four depends critically on previous nutrition and health conditions and that this early measure is an accurate predictor of adult height.

The benefits of better health show up in schooling. Healthier children attend school more regularly and are more able to keep up with schoolwork—and both advantages improve their performance in school. In Jamaica children infected with whipworm scored 15 percent lower before treatment than did their uninfected schoolmates. After treatment they did almost as well as the uninfected children.

The health of adults also affects children's schooling. An adult's death or sickness may precipitate a child's withdrawal from school. The loss of household income may make it more difficult for the family to afford the costs of schooling. And the child may have to take over household responsibilities previously performed by the sick or dead person—problems compounded by the spread of AIDS.

Investing in People

IN 1990 MORE THAN THREE-QUARTERS OF THE WORLD'S 540 MILlion children of primary school age were in school, compared with 69 percent a decade earlier. Coverage of secondary and higher education also has expanded. And health indicators have improved significantly. In 1960 child mortality exceeded 175 deaths per thousand children age one to four in most of the developing world. By 1990 such high rates persisted mainly in parts of Africa.

This success is not cause for complacency. Progress has been uneven across countries—and across groups within countries. The number of primary-school-age children not enrolled in school remains large—130 million in 1990, most of them in low-income countries and low-income families. In each cohort of children who began school in the late 1980s in developing countries, fewer than 80 percent stayed through their fourth year, and only 67 percent completed the primary cycle. Because of poor schooling conditions, large numbers of students leave school with poor academic achievement—and fail as adults to reap the full benefits of having been to school.

Nearly half of all early childhood deaths stem from diseases for which inexpensive prevention and treatment exist.

In health, too, more remains to be done. About 12 million children under the age of five died in the developing world in 1990. A quarter of these deaths were linked—directly or in association with infectious diseases—to inadequate diets. Nearly half of all early childhood deaths stem from diarrheal diseases, acute respiratory infection, measles, and malaria—problems for which inexpensive and easily administered prevention and treatment exist. Deaths among young children also arise from poorly timed pregnancies. Surveys in 25 developing countries suggest that, if closely spaced births were delayed until mothers wanted them, child mortality in those countries might be reduced by 20 percent.

Among adults communicable diseases remain all too common. Malaria and tuberculosis are on the rise, made worse by the evolution of drug-resistant microbes. In the past decade AIDS has emerged as a serious new health threat, and in Sub-Saharan Africa the epidemic could easily reverse past gains in life expectancy. In most of the developing world aging populations pose additional challenges in increasing burdens of noncommunicable diseases, such as heart attacks, strokes, and ill health associated with high consumption of alcohol and tobacco.

Governments thus have a responsibility to invest in the education and health of their people. The best results are achieved by governments that channel public resources to basic education and health services—and pay attention to the needs of low-income people and other disadvantaged groups. Governments can act as catalysts in mobilizing private contributions for the development of human capital—notably by facilitating diversity and competition in the financing and provision of services. And they can promote the development of the education and health sectors by disseminating essential information on provider performance, setting up transparent regulatory frameworks for private sector activity, and creating student finance and health insurance schemes.

Education

PUBLIC SPENDING ON EDUCATION IS SUBSTANTIAL IN MOST countries, accounting for at least half of all spending on education in low-income countries and 70 to 80 percent in middle- and upper-income countries. It is often the largest single item in public budgets, representing on average 16 percent of government spending in developing countries in 1990, or 4.3 percent of national income. There is no theoretically appropriate share of GNP or public spending that should be devoted to education. But many countries could achieve more educational attainment with the same—or even less—public spending, by focusing spending on the lower levels of education and increasing efficiency of resource use and by relying more on private financing at the higher levels.

Many countries could achieve more educational attainment with the same—or even less—public spending.

To emphasize the point about using resources efficiently, compare public spending on education as a percentage of GNP with gross enrollment ratios for a number of countries (figure 1). Despite the limitations of using gross enrollment ratios, such an international comparison helps to identify countries where public spending appears to stimulate relatively low levels of human capital formation. Mauritania and Morocco, for example, show particularly poor results, despite high public spending on education. Their public spending on education is very inefficient compared with that of Jamaica and Jordan. Similarly, Cameroon, El Salvador, and Thailand are inefficient compared with Ecuador and Syria. Such comparisons also show how public spending in some countries is very low compared with international averages. In Guatemala, for example, public spending appears to be relatively efficient compared with spending in Mauritania and Senegal which have worse outcomes but devote a larger share of GNP to public spending on education. In some African countries resources are allocated so inefficiently that the current generation of school children is projected to attain only a half to a third as many years of schooling as children in other African countries with comparable public spending on education and per capita GNP.

Figure 1 Higher Public Spending on Education Does Not Always Mean Higher Human Capital Formation

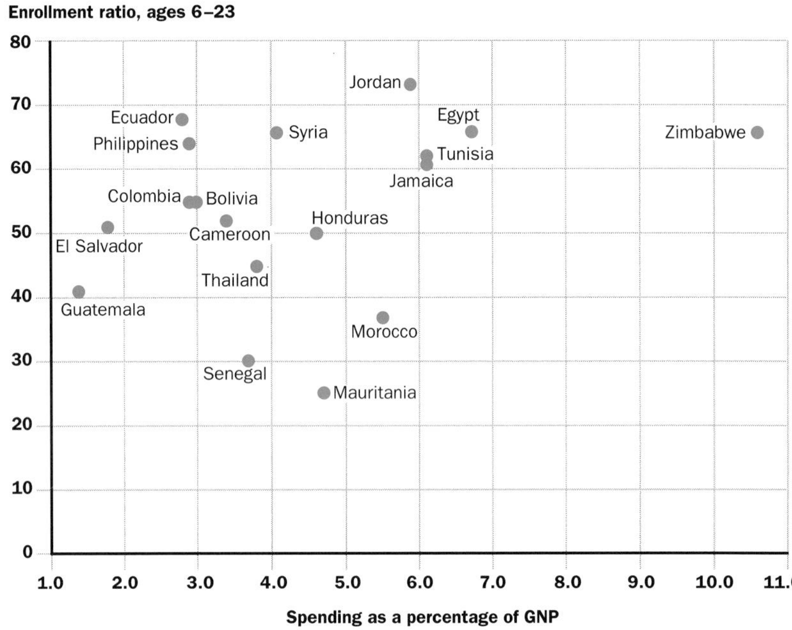

Note: Graph includes countries with per capita GNP between US$500 and US$1,500 in 1990.
Source: Mingat and Tan (1994).

Highly subsidized higher education typically absorbs much public spending, leaving little for primary schooling—a common misallocation of resources. In Mauritania 57 percent of public spending on higher education goes for student aid, and in Senegal, 44 percent. In India, too, the bulk of public spending on education has gone to support heavily subsidized higher education. This pattern is inequitable—because students in higher education typically come from the highest income groups. It is also wasteful—because the subsidies displace private spending.

Increasing the private financing of higher education may be politically unpalatable, but experience from several countries shows that it can be done. Between 1980 and 1990 the share of recurrent higher education costs funded from tuition charges rose from 23 percent to 43 percent in Korea, from zero to 21 percent in Viet Nam, from 13 percent to 25 percent in Mexico, and from 8 percent to 16 percent in Costa Rica. When coupled with selective scholarships and student loans, tuition increases need not hurt deserving students from low-income families.

Redirecting spending toward primary education is only a first step toward better education outcomes—the resources must also be used effectively. The quality of schooling can be improved in many countries with increased investments in textbooks and other learning materials. Improving the physical conditions of primary schools also is a priority, particularly where lack of sanitary facilities is likely to discourage parents from sending girls to school. Further, in some settings providing scholarships can encourage low-income parents to enroll their children, especially daughters. Other promising avenues for improvement include early childhood education, periodic in-service teacher training, and interactive radio instruction to supplement teaching when teachers lack knowledge of the subject.

Governments can expand access to education by lifting bans on private education. In Tanzania this simple measure alone led to an explosive growth in secondary enrollments, so much so that private schools now enroll more students than public schools. Since most of the new schools are self-financing, the expansion of education opportunities costs the government little. Within the public school system there are advantages in decentralizing and delegating decisionmaking to communities and schools.

Governments can expand access to education by lifting bans on private education.

Educating girls is key to moving from a vicious cycle of ignorance, disease, and poverty to a virtuous cycle of learning, skills, better nutrition, good health, and sustainable development. Because the barriers to girls' education are usually cultural, religious, and economic, a variety of approaches is needed to break them down (box 8).

Health

DEVELOPING COUNTRIES SPEND ALMOST 5 PERCENT OF THEIR national income on health, half from the government. As in education, countries vary substantially in the efficiency with which they deploy resources. Very often, there is little or no relation between the resources expended and the health outcomes achieved (figure 2). By focusing resources on basic services, China, for example, spends a full percentage point less of its GDP than other countries at the

Box 8 Improving Girls' Access to Education

THE BEST WAY TO IMPROVE EDUCATION FOR girls is to improve education for all, because girls' access to formal education increases as overall educational opportunities increase. Experience during the 1980s in such countries as Burundi, Senegal, Uganda, and Zimbabwe shows that improving access to education for all increases girls' share in enrollment.

In many primary schools dropout and repetition rates are high, so that countries must pay for as many as nine years of education to produce one pupil who has completed the fifth grade. This inefficiency, accounting for as much as 30 percent of many primary education budgets, is something few nations can afford if they are to improve educational quality—and especially if they are to increase access to education for girls.

But no country with low female enrollment can rely solely on this general approach to increase educational access and quality. It will not redress the imbalance against girls quickly enough. There must also be specific targeting.

One basic policy instrument is to increase school places specifically for girls. If there are too few school places, the scarce places often are first allocated to boys. Bangladesh, Chad, India, Pakistan, Senegal, and Yemen all have made special efforts to extend classrooms or build new schools exclusively for girls.

A second policy instrument is to reserve some school places for girls—as has been done in Malawi, where the government reserves a third of all secondary school places for girls. Tanzania has a similar policy.

Adding school places may not be sufficient if the demand from parents and the community is lacking. In Bangladesh, Chad, Mali, Morocco, Pakistan, and Papua New Guinea World Bank-assisted projects have included information campaigns on this topic.

Other programs for targeting and increasing girls' access to education include:

- Hiring more female teachers to draw more girls into school.
- Offering special scholarship programs for girls living in rural areas—such as those begun in Bangladesh and Guatemala.
- Offering flexible school hours that allow girls to combine schooling with household chores, to address the opportunity cost of girls' school attendance.
- Protecting girls' privacy to reassure parents. The effectiveness of this approach has been demonstrated in Pakistan, where appropriate sanitary facilities and boundary walls around girls' schools have been provided.
- Building child care centers at or near schools to relieve girls of the responsibility of caring for siblings during the day.
- Measures outside the education sector also can promote female schooling. In Nepal the government distributed fuel-efficient, smokeless, wood-burning stoves to 15,000 families as part of a program to check deforestation. This reduced the time spent by girls collecting wood for cooking—which in turn increased girls' enrollments. In Morocco girls' enrollments were significantly higher in communities with tapped water than elsewhere.

same stage of development (measured by GDP and level of education), but it achieves 10 years of additional life expectancy. By contrast, Malawi spends a full two percentage points more of its GDP on health than comparable countries, but life expectancy there is five years shorter.

There are good reasons for government intervention in health in general and in some specific areas. The control of infectious diseases (tuberculosis, for example) is important because it has wider benefits for society

Figure 2 Public Spending and Life Expectancy: How Resources Are Allocated Matters More Than How Much Is Spent

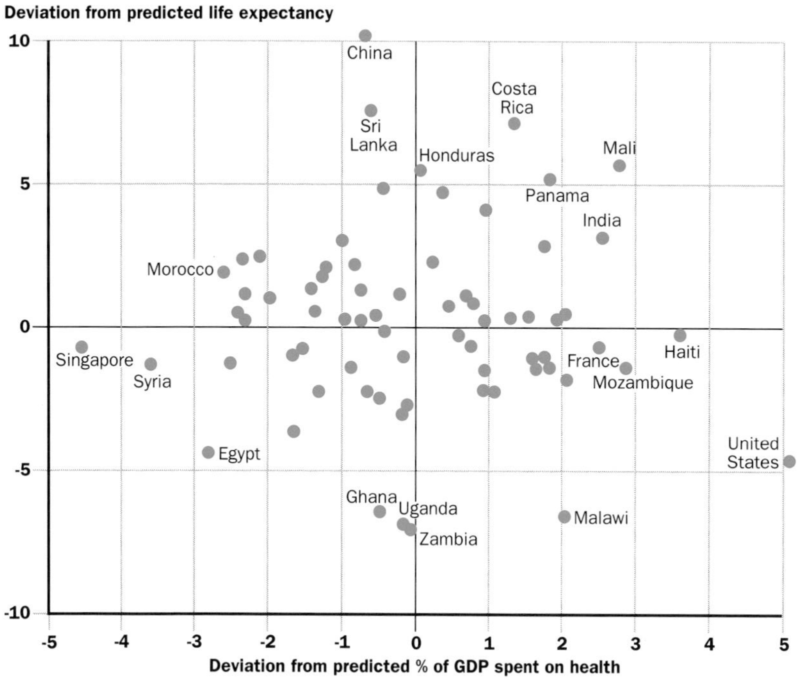

Source: 1993 World Development Report.

and because, if successful, it will help the poor disproportionately. There also is a case for government investment in sanitation and safe drinking water, as the benefits, particularly of improved sanitation, go well beyond the immediate users' environment. Unsanitary conditions and unclean water are responsible for some of the diseases that afflict mostly poor people. In such areas as the prevention of illnesses that affect children or the provision of family planning services, public support is justified because of information failures. The systematic underestimation of the value of child immunization, for example, has been well documented.

To improve health conditions, governments need to redirect resources toward services that confer benefits on the largest number of people. They can do this by supporting:

Control of infectious diseases helps the poor disproportionately.

- Essential public health services, such as immunization, AIDS prevention, school-based health services (including micronutrient

Governments need to redirect resources toward services that benefit the largest number of people.

supplementation), information and selected services for family planning, programs to reduce tobacco and alcohol consumption, and regulatory action, information, and selective public investments to encourage healthy home environments (clean water, sanitation, garbage collection).

- A package of essential clinical services, whose comprehensiveness and composition depend on each country's epidemiological conditions, preferences, and income. At a minimum, the package should include prenatal care, family planning services, tuberculosis control, control of sexually transmitted diseases, care of the most common serious illnesses affecting children, and some treatment for minor infections.

Together, the two packages of services could cost $12 per person a year in low-income countries (or 3.4 percent of per capita income) and $22 per person a year in middle-income countries (or 0.9 percent of per capita income). Many countries would find these costs affordable if they were to display greater commitment to reducing military expenditure and shifting resources away from services that mostly benefit the well-to-do.

Better management also is essential for better results. In the public sector such measures as decentralizing administrative and budgetary authority and contracting out services can reduce costs without compromising service delivery. Outside the public sector the government needs to encourage the development of regulated social and private insurance to cover clinical services not in the package of publicly funded services. The government also can facilitate competition among suppliers of clinical services and drugs to expand consumer choice and keep a lid on costs.

Taking Advantage of Intersectoral Relationships

IMPORTANT LINKS AMONG THE DIFFERENT AREAS OF HUMAN resource investments can and should be exploited to extract the most benefit from each dollar spent. The incomes of the poor significantly affect their health, education, nutrition, and fertility. Poor people cannot afford decent food and health care, and they are likely to have larger families to ensure that they will be supported during their old age or if they become disabled. They also are more likely to require that children enter the labor market or help around the home, preventing them from attending school. Public policies on education, health, nutrition, and population can help liberate people from these tendencies.

Education is one of the single most important determinants of individuals' health and life expectancy.

Education is one of the single most important determinants of individual health and life expectancy. The causal relationship tends to be cyclical: as more educated individuals make investments in their health and therefore live longer, their improved life expectancy motivates them to make still further investments in their education and health. Parents (especially mothers) with a primary education are more likely to follow good health, hygiene, and nutrition practices, improving overall household welfare. Educating mothers also is the most crucial factor in lowering fertility. Educated mothers are more likely to have the independence to decide on the size of their families and to use modern contraceptives and seek family planning advice. As a mother's education and her subsequent earning potential increase, the cost of having a child goes up. Better-educated women marry and start their families later, diminishing the risk of ill health associated with early pregnancies. Not only do educated parents have fewer children, but the benefits for each child's welfare are compounded by the fact that these families then invest more per child.

Improved health status and a longer life expectancy within families also play a key role in lowering fertility; parents tend to have fewer children when the odds are greater that their children will survive. Although it is possible (though not firmly established) that better nutrition may increase natural fecundity, its effects on the health, education, and incomes of the poor all contribute indirectly to reducing fertility.

Another interrelationship is that better nutrition improves a child's capacity to learn. Studies consistently show that malnutrition is related to low cognitive test scores and school performance. Health and nutrition both affect whether children can attend school regularly enough to reach a useful level of attainment and whether they have the mental and physical alertness and capacity to learn. Micronutrient malnutrition not only can decrease a child's alertness and capacity to learn, but also can impede brain development and increase the chances of a child's developing blindness. Malnutrition and disease have been found to be closely connected, each increasing the likelihood and severity of the other (box 9).

A strategic approach to human resource development therefore requires careful assessment of all the benefits from a given intervention. It also calls for a willingness to reach across sectors. Developing human capital by itself is not enough—that must go hand in hand with the in-

Box 9 Early Childhood Development

IT IS A VICIOUS CIRCLE. MALNOURISHED MOTHERS GIVE BIRTH to low-birthweight babies, who become the most likely candidates for malnutrition. More than a million children are blind because they do not get enough vitamin A. An estimated 50 million are seriously impaired mentally and physically because their diets lack iodine. More than half of young children in poor countries are anemic. What must be done to break the cycle of poverty?

Some of the most serious problems faced by the young (measles, dehydration, polio, pneumonia, tetanus, intestinal parasites, and most malnutrition)—can now be prevented relatively easily and at low cost. Vitamin A can be provided for about 50 cents a child a year, and iodine—by fortifying salt—for 5 cents. It would cost only about $15 per head to immunize children in low-income countries against seven of the most dangerous diseases. Inexpensive but effective methods of nutrition and health education could make major contributions. More attention also is critically needed for integrated early childhood development programs that include intellectual and social stimulation and related child care, along with nutrition and health programs, so that preschool-age children can develop properly and be better able to cope with formal primary schooling. Evidence indicates that well-designed and well-implemented programs at the preschool level can over time increase the efficiency of investments in primary and secondary education, contribute to children's future productivity and income, and reduce the costs of providing social services over the long run.

troduction of sound economic policies. Policy failures largely explain the low returns to much of the post-independence investment in education and health in many African countries. The key is to improve the interaction between human capital and complementary factors of production—and that requires good policies.

Four Priorities for Action

AROUND THE WORLD MUCH HAS ALREADY BEEN DONE TO increase investments in human capital. As in the past, governments will continue to play a major role in bringing about sustained progress. But results do not depend only on additional resources. They also depend on how well those resources are used, how successfully intersectoral links are exploited, and how effectively the government catalyzes, rather than undermines, private effort. Evidence from research and experience in human development over the past few decades suggests four priorities for action.

- *Invest in basic education.* In the poorest countries this typically means focusing on primary education. Where primary enrollments are universal, the emphasis shifts toward secondary education. At both levels the aim is to expand access and improve learning outcomes.
- *Invest in girls' education.* This is one area where cross-sectoral linkages can be exploited to great advantage—because educating girls is one of the most socially productive investments that governments can support. Even if an educated woman never enters the labor market, her increased productivity materializes in lower fertility and improved child and maternal health—bringing benefits that far exceed the cost of her education.
- *Invest in cost-effective health services.* Many governments can achieve better returns by channeling public spending away from high-cost services used mainly by the rich and toward more cost-effective interventions that attack the major sources of a country's burden of disease. Priorities include eliminating malnutrition, ensuring access to the minimum package of essential public health and clinical services, and facilitating the avoidance of unwanted and poorly spaced births.
- *Invest in early childhood development.* Integrated programs of nutrition, health, and education interventions are the best for meeting the diverse needs of very young children. Social and intellectual stimulation, along with nutrition and health services, can improve child welfare, increase the efficiency of investments in primary and secondary education, and reduce the cost of social services in the long run.

By focusing public efforts in these areas, and by establishing an appropriate framework for expanded private sector activity in financing and delivering social services, governments can be effective catalysts for future progress. Although the need for tuning the approach to country conditions is obvious, the thrust of action is common—because investing in people is essential to achieving economic and social progress.

Governments can be catalysts for progress.

CHAPTER 7

The World Bank and Social Development

ECONOMIC AND SOCIAL DEVELOPMENT IS AT THE core of the World Bank's mandate, which is to help countries reduce poverty and improve living standards through sustainable growth and investments in people. Achieving growth requires harnessing market incentives, building social and economic institutions, developing infrastructure, protecting the environment, and mastering technology. Investing in people means providing basic social services of universal reach and adequate quality: primary education, essential health care, family planning, and nutrition programs.

The World Bank's mandate is to help countries reduce poverty and improve living standards through sustainable growth and investments in people.

Sound policies, investments in physical and human capital, and effective public institutions are essential for development. But that is not all. Development must be people-oriented and include efforts to reduce inequality and better manage economic change. In this regard the Bank is increasingly emphasizing improved governance, which is essential for sound economic management and social stability. Under its mandate the Bank draws a clear distinction between economic and political dimensions of governance and limits its work to the economic.

The Bank's support concentrates on four areas: improving *public sector management,* including civil service reform, public financial management, and public enterprise reform; devising strategies for improving pubic sector *accountability,* including decentralization, increased beneficiary participation in projects, and increased private competition in service delivery; encouraging greater *transparency and increased flow of information;* and supporting development of the *legal and regulatory framework* for economic activity (laws on property rights, foreign investment, bankruptcy, and competition). The primary focus of World

Bank activities, however, remains helping countries reduce widespread poverty, malnutrition, hunger, and illiteracy.

The Bank has contributed to the economic and social progress of the past 50 years by supporting more than 6,000 operations in 140 countries with more than $300 billion in financing. The strategy that the Bank advises countries to follow in order to improve living standards centers on promoting labor-demanding growth, investing in people, providing safety nets, and improving governance. To help countries implement the strategy, the Bank uses a variety of instruments. Each instrument is designed to contribute toward the overall goal of reducing poverty. But no single instrument can bring about sustained poverty reduction. That requires a combination of instruments. And as will become clear, structural adjustment is only one of the instruments that the Bank employs in its efforts to help countries reduce poverty.

One of the main instruments that the Bank relies on is policy advice and technical assistance, to support the efforts of developing countries to make policy and institutional adjustments in response to changing domestic and international developments. In the early 1980s, when it became clear that countries trying to adapt to the external shocks of the 1970s needed financial support beyond project lending, the Bank introduced adjustment lending. Economic reform programs supported by the Bank, in collaboration with the International Monetary Fund (IMF), have evolved to cover not just short-term stabilization but improvements in long-term economic management, safety nets for the poor, restructuring of public expenditure in favor of the social sectors, public sector institution-building, and private sector development.

Despite the important role of adjustment lending in the late 1980s and early 1990s, the bulk of Bank lending has always supported specific investment projects. And in recent years adjustment operations have diminished to less than 15 percent of total Bank lending. World Bank investment projects support development activities in many sectors. But in recognition of the growing awareness of the importance of human capital in raising living standards, the Bank in recent years has dramatically increased investments in people—from about 5 percent of total lending in the early 1980s to 15 percent in 1994. The composition of those investments also is changing, with more emphasis on primary education, girls' education, and primary health care. The Bank now lends more than $2 billion a year for education, $1 billion for health, and $200 million for population activities, making it the world's largest fi-

The World Bank is now the world's largest financing source for investments in people.

nancing source for investments in people. It also is the largest lender for programs to combat a disease devastating the economic potential of some developing countries—AIDS—with total lending now approaching $600 million. The Bank's lending for human resources development is expected to grow, to $15 billion over the next three years.

Both project lending and lending in support of policy reforms are directed at the same basic goal of reducing poverty. But beyond the general quest for poverty reduction, some Bank-financed projects are targeted at specific groups of poor or disadvantaged people, including unskilled workers, women, the old, migrants, residents of less developed regions, low-income households in urban areas, and people from particular ethnic groups (box 10). Project interventions targeted at the poor have as their main objective raising productivity, developing human resources, improving access to safe drinking water and proper sanitation, and providing safety nets. During 1992–94 the Bank committed almost $13 billion to a large number of projects that directly target the poor.

Some Bank-supported programs of policy reform also focus on issues of special relevance to poverty reduction. Seventeen of the 23 adjustment operations approved in 1994 fall into this category. To qualify as poverty-focused, adjustment operations must include one or more of the following measures: restructuring public expenditure to shift resources toward the basic economic and social services that most benefit the poor, removing distortions that adversely affect the poor (such as controls on producer prices of crops), targeting specific programs (labor-intensive public works, nutrition programs) at the poor, and setting up a mechanism for poverty monitoring.

From time to time the Bank also is called on to lend for postwar reconstruction—something that is vital to social integration generally and to the reintegration of refugees into mainstream society in particular. Aimed at facilitating the transition from war to peace, Bank lending is usually directed at rehabilitating basic transport and water infrastructure, increasing the availability of basic educational and medical supplies, and improving the supply of imported intermediate inputs to industries producing basic commodities. Countries that have benefitted from this type of assistance include Cambodia, Ethiopia, Uganda, and, more recently, Rwanda.

The Bank always endeavors to tailor its assistance—whether policy advice, technical assistance, project lending, or loans in support of policy reforms—to the circumstances of each country. It is the same with

Box 10 Project Lending: Targeted Interventions

PROGRAMS TARGETED AT THE POOR AND DISADVANTAGED CAN address a variety of needs, including raising the productivity of the poor, supporting development in very poor regions, ensuring access to services for indigenous people, and providing safety nets.

Raising the productivity of the poor. Kenya's *Micro and Small Enterprise Training and Technology Project* has established a training fund for skill upgrading and technology development for micro- and small enterprises, with vouchers being distributed to entrepreneurs with low income and provisions made for promoting women entrepreneurs. The *Mozambique Second Roads and Coastal Shipping Project* is designed to open up agricultural areas where poor small farmers live, to lower the cost to the poor of accessing markets and increase farmers' incomes and employment opportunities.

Supporting development in the poorest regions. In Tunisia the *Northwest Mountainous Areas Development Project* will promote sustainable agricultural productivity, erosion control, and rural infrastructure in isolated, impoverished mountainous regions, as well as rural enterprises that would not be financed by existing formal credit schemes. In Indonesia the *Semarang-Surakarta Urban Development Project* aims to provide better access to essential services and an improved urban environment for the poor through improved roads, additional water supply, improved drainage, market improvements, basic housing rehabilitation for slum areas, and expanded coverage of sanitation, sewerage and solid waste collection.

Addressing the needs of indigenous groups. The *Paraguay Natural Resources Management Project* would provide assistance to indigenous groups by regularizing land tenancy and expanding their land areas, supporting diversification and increases in output in order to reduce dependency on paid work, improving their health care, and promoting primary and informal education.

Supporting safety nets. The *Ecuador Third Social Development Fund*, the *Peru Social Development and Compensation Fund*, and the *Pakistan Social Action Program* all provide funds for community-based social assistance programs. The *Albania Technical Assistance Project*, which provides assistance to the government to reform the social protection system, will include measures to protect needy groups, such as the unemployed, during the economic transition period.

the level and composition of its lending. Through consultations with government and the private sector, and with the aid of in-depth studies, the Bank tries to understand a country's development objectives and policies and the internal and external constraints on its development. This is not always easy, because in some countries there are severe data limitations. In these cases the Bank also works with governments to improve the capacity of the statistical services to collect and process data.

There is scope for using public expenditure reviews more effectively in policy dialogue with governments.

Increasingly, the Bank is carrying out detailed household-level studies on poverty in an effort to learn more about who the poor are, what types of activities they engage in, what social services they have access to, and how different policies affect them. These studies usually result in the definition of a poverty line, which helps to distinguish the poor from the nonpoor, based on measures of income or expenditure. There is a clear need for this type of analysis in more countries, to determine the conditions of the poor at a particular point in time and changes in poverty over time. This work is being done as the results of more household surveys become available. Efforts also are being made to involve poor people in the process of poverty analysis.

The Bank also carries out public expenditure reviews, in cooperation with governments and other donors. These reviews help focus attention on the need to keep the overall level of public expenditures consistent with maintaining macroeconomic stability. In some instances the reviews have been used to initiate a restructuring of public expenditures to focus them on high- priority programs that promote economic growth and human resource development. But there is still scope for using the results of public expenditure reviews more effectively in policy dialogue with governments. In many countries there is room for reallocation of resources between sectors (say, from defense to the social sectors) and within sectors (from hospital-based curative care to public health measures, for example).

Development must take into account the needs of future generations as well as those of the present generation. That is why environmental protection is important. Without it, long-term development is undermined. At the same time, without development it is not possible to generate the resources needed for environmental protection. The Bank seeks to build on this link by supporting projects for afforestation, pollution control, and land management. It also invests in water, sanitation, and agricultural extension to help the poor deal with some of the environmental problems they face. And it has put in place processes for

Without environmental protection, long-term development is undermined.

The Bank will continue to increase lending for investments in people and for improvements in governance.

assessing the potential environmental impact of the projects it finances, so that plans can be drawn up to mitigate the adverse effects that are identified. The Bank also is trying out social assessments, to analyze the social impact of projects. These assessments are being carried out in a number of countries and more are planned.

In advancing economic and social development, the Bank will continue to deepen its understanding of developments in individual countries and in the global economy. It will build on its two main roles—lender and advisor. It will continue to mobilize and invest substantial resources for development, paying more attention to the needs of the poor, to the allocation of public expenditure, and to the environmental and social impact of projects. The combination of its financial and advisory roles gives the Bank Group its comparative advantage. While these roles will continue to be performed primarily at the country level, the Bank will do more to distill and disseminate its cross-country experience and to connect clients with the best available knowledge from other sources. It also will respond, as in the past, to shareholder requests to help address strategic development issues that transcend national boundaries.

The Bank's work in helping countries pursue economic reforms will be geared closely to the different phases of economic reform in which different borrowers find themselves. The Bank will continue to help governments implement policy reforms and assist with the provision of social safety nets to mitigate their transitional costs. And it will continue to increase lending for investments in people and for improvements in governance.

In human resources the Bank will give high priority to reaching disadvantaged young children in the developing world. Early nutrition, health, and education interventions to protect and develop the human potential of disadvantaged children are critical to break the cycle of poverty. Bank efforts will focus on situations in which deprivation is most severe and on countries in which it affects the most people. It will work with its key partners on this program.

The Bank will continue to play an active role in mobilizing resources and in coordinating donor efforts in support of particular countries. Given the scale and scope of the development agenda, the Bank Group must be careful to avoid stretching itself too thin. In line with its recent Vision paper, the Bank will focus more on doing what it does best while encouraging a more sensible division of labor within the international development community. To this end, the Bank will strengthen strategic alliances with its partners in development, drawing on the comparative advantage of each organization. In particular, it will:

- work in partnership with borrowing countries, donor countries, and international development agencies to carry out the social development agenda agreed at the Copenhagen Summit.
- with other agencies, support institutional development and capacity-building in borrowing countries, and promote greater local involvement in the design, preparation, and supervision of Bank-financed projects, programs and studies.
- with other donors, encourage micro-enterprises and small-scale environmental initiatives, through local intermediaries.
- in collaboration with UN agencies and other donors, improve baseline information on poverty and developing countries' capacity to monitor their progress in reducing poverty.

The goal is to improve the lives of people everywhere.

The goal of economic and social development is to improve the lives of people everywhere—reducing widespread poverty, spreading opportunities for more productive work, and pulling societies together for the equitable and participatory advancement of common purposes.

Selected Bibliography

Becker, Gary. 1994. "Human Capital and Poverty Alleviation." Interim transcript of a lecture at the World Bank. Washington, D.C.

Berg, Elliot, Graeme Hunter, Tom Lenaghan, and Malaika Riley. 1994. *Poverty and Structural Adjustment in the 1980s: Trends in Welfare Indicators in Latin America and Africa.* A study prepared for the U.S. Agency for International Development, Bureau for Private Enterprise, Office of Small, Micro and Informal Enterprise. Bethesda, Md.: Development Alternatives Incorporated.

Bhatnagar, Bhuvan, and Aubrey Williams, eds. 1993. *Participatory Development and the World Bank: Potential Directions for Change.* World Bank Discussion Paper 183. Washington, D.C.

Birdsall, Nancy, and Richard Sabot. 1994. "Virtuous Circles: Human Capital, Growth, and Equity in East Asia." World Bank, Policy Research Department, Washington, D.C.

Cornia, Andrea, Frances Stewart, and Richard Jolly. 1987. *Adjustment with a Human Face.* A Study by UNICEF. New York: Oxford University Press.

Cornia, Andrea, Rolph van der Hoeven, and Thandika Mkandawire. 1992. *Africa's Recovery in the 1990s.* A Study by UNICEF. New York: St. Martin's Press.

Cox Edwards, Alejandra, and Sebastian Edwards. 1990. "Labor Market Distortions and Structural Adjustment in Developing Countries." NBER Working Paper 3346. National Bureau of Economic Research, Cambridge, Mass.

Demery, Lionel, Binayak Sen, and Tara Vishwanath. 1994. "Poverty, Inequality and Growth." World Bank, Education and Social Policy Department, Washington, D.C.

Dia, Mamadou. 1993. "Position Paper for Improving Civil Service Efficiency in Sub-Saharan Africa." World Bank, Africa Technical Department, Washington, D.C.

Fishlow, Albert, Catherine Gwin, Stephen Haggard, Dani Rodrik, and Robert Wade. 1994. *Miracle or Design? Lessons from the East Asian Experience.* Policy Essay 11. Washington, D.C.: Overseas Development Council.

Fogel, R. 1993. "The Relevance of Malthus for the Study of Mortality Today." Working paper. University of Chicago, Chicago.

Glewwe, Paul, and Dennis de Tray. 1989. *The Poor in Latin America During Adjustment: A Case Study of Peru.* Living Standards Measurement Study Working Paper 56. Washington, D.C.: World Bank.

Graham, Carol. 1994. *Safety Nets, Politics, and the Poor: Transitions to Market Economies.* Washington, D.C.: The Brookings Institution.

Grosh, Margaret. 1990a. "The Jamaican Food Stamps Program: A Case Study." World Bank, Human Resources Division, Washington, D.C.

Grosh, Margaret. 1990b. *Social Spending in Latin America, the Story of the 1980s.* World Bank Discussion Paper 106. Washington, D.C.

Gulhati, Ravi, and Raj Nallari. 1990. *Successful Stabilization and Recovery in Mauritius.* EDI Analytical Case Study 5. Washington, D.C.: World Bank.

Horton, Susan, Ravi Kanbur, and Dipak Mazumdar. 1990. "Labor Markets in an Era of Adjustment: An Overview." Policy Research Working Paper 694. World Bank, Washington, D.C.

Hossain, Shaik. 1994. "Education Finance: Public and Private Sector Interface."

Husain, Ishrat. 1991. "How Did the Asian Countries Avoid the Debt Crisis?" Policy Research Working Paper 785. World Bank, Washington, D.C.

Jalan, Jyotsna, and Kalanidhi Subbarao. Forthcoming. "Adjustment and Social Sectors in India." in R. Cassen and V. Jushi, eds., *India: The Future of Economic Reform.*

Jamison, Dean. 1986. "Child Malnutrition and School Retardation in China." *Journal of Development Economics,* 20.

Jarousse, Jean-Pierre, and Alain Mingat. 1992. "Options for Accelerated Development of Primary Education in the Sahel." World Bank, Washington, D.C.

Jolly, Richard, and Giovanni Cornia, eds. 1984. *The Impact of Recession on Children: A Study Prepared for UNICEF.* Oxford: Oxford University Press.

Kakwani, Nanak and Kalanidhi Subbarao. 1993. "Rural Poverty in India." In Michael Lipton and Jacques van der Gaag, eds. *Including the Poor.* World Bank Regional and Sectoral Study, Washington, D.C.

Kakwani, Nanak, Elene Makonnen, and Jacques van der Gaag. 1990. "Structural Adjustment and Living Conditions in Developing Countries." Policy Research Working Paper 467. World Bank, Washington, D.C.

Kanbur, Ravi, and Marco Ferroni. 1990. *Poverty-Conscious Restructuring of Public Expenditures.* Social Dimensions of Adjustment in Sub-Saharan Africa Working Paper 9. Washington, D.C.: World Bank.

Killick, Tony. 1993. *The Adaptive Economy: Adjustment Policies in Small, Low-Income Countries.* EDI Development Study. Washington, D.C.: World Bank.

Larsson, Karl-Anders. 1994. *Structural Adjustment: Aid and Development.* Stockholm: SIDA.

Lau, L.J., D.T. Jamison, S-C. Liu, and S. Rivkin. 1993. "Education and Economic Growth: Some Cross-Sectional Evidence from Brazil." *Journal of Development Economics* 41:45–70.

Lele, Uma. 1989. *Structural Adjustment, Agricultural Development and the Poor: Lessons from the Malawian Experience.* MADIA Discussion Paper 9. Washington, D.C.: World Bank.

Lockheed, Marlaine, and Adriaan Verspoor and associates. 1991. *Improving Primary Education in Developing Countries.* New York: Oxford University Press.

Mingat, Alain and Jee-Peng Tan. 1994. "International Perspectives on Education: Some Ideas for Data Analysis." World Bank, Education and Social Policy Department, Washington, D.C.

Omari, Issa. 1994. "Education Sector Review Paper." Dar es Salaam.

Ozorio de Almeida, A.L., and Scott Graham. 1994. "Regulatory Costs and Employment in the Informal Sector in Argentina." Education and Social Policy Discussion Paper 45. World Bank, Washington, D.C.

Patrinos, Harry. 1994. "Notes on Education and Economic Growth: Theory and Evidence." HRO Policy Working Paper 39. World Bank, Human Resources Development and Operations Policy, Washington, D.C.

Pradhan, S., and V. Swaroop. 1993. "Public Spending and Adjustment." *Finance and Development.*

Psacharopoulos, George, Samuel Morley, Ariel Fizbein, Haeduck Lee, and Bill Wood. 1993. *Poverty and Income Distribution in Latin America: The Story of the 1980s.* Washington, D.C.: World Bank.

Putnam, Robert, with Leonardi Robert and Yanetti Raffaella. 1993. *Making Democracy Work: Civic Traditions in Modern Italy.* Princeton, N.J.: Princeton University Press

Quisumbing, Agnes R. 1993. "Gender Differences in Agricultural Productivity: A Survey of Empirical Evidence." Background paper. World Bank, Education and Social Policy Department, Washington, D.C.

Ravallion, Martin, and Monica Huppi. 1991. "Measuring Changes in Poverty: A Methodological Case Study of Indonesia during an Adjustment Period." *World Bank Economic Review* 5 (1): 57–82.

Ravallion, Martin, Gaurav Datt, Dominique van de Walle, and Elaine Chan. 1991. "Quantifying the Magnitude and Severity of Absolute Poverty in the Developing World in the Mid-1980s." Policy Research Working Paper 587. World Bank, Washington, D.C.

Ribe, Helena, and Soniya Carvalho. 1990. "World Bank Treatment of the Social Impact of Adjustment Programs." Policy Research Working Paper 521. World Bank, Washington, D.C.

Ribe, Helena, Soniya Carvalho, Robert Liebenthal, Peter Nicholas, and Elaine Zuckerman. 1990. *How Adjustment Programs Can Help the Poor: The World Bank Experience.* World Bank Discussion Paper 71. Washington, D.C.

Sahn, David E. 1992. "Public Expenditures in Sub-Saharan Africa During a Period of Economic Reforms." *World Development* 20 (May): 673–93.

Schiff, Maurice, and Alberto Valdes. 1992. *Plundering of Agriculture in Developing Countries.* Washington, D.C.: World Bank.

Schultz, T. Paul, and Aysit Tansel. 1993. "Estimates of Wage Returns to Adult Health in Côte d'Ivoire and Ghana." Yale University, New Haven.

Serageldin, Ismail, and Pierre Landell-Mills. 1992. "Governance and the External Factor." In *Proceedings of the World Bank Conference on Development Economics.* 1991. Washington, D.C.

Subbarao, Kalanidhi, Jeanine Braithwaite, and Jyotsna Jalan. 1994. "Protecting the Poor during Adjustment and Transitions." World Bank, Education and Social Policy Department, Washington, D.C.

Subbarao, Kalinidhi, and Kene Ezemanari. 1993. "Transition, Poverty and Social Assistance in Mongolia." World Bank, Education and Social Policy Department, Washington, D.C.

Summers, Lawrence H. 1992. "Investing in All the People." Policy Research Working Paper 905. World Bank, Development Economics, Office of the Vice President, Washington, D.C.

Tan, Jee-Pang, and Alain Mingat. 1992. *Education in Asia: A Comparative Study of Cost and Financing.* World Bank Regional and Sectoral Study. Washington, D.C.

ul Haq, Mabub. 1994. "New Imperatives of Human Security." A Policy Paper commissioned by the UNDP for the World Summit for Social Development. UNDP, New York.

UNESCO (United Nations Educational, Scientific, and Cultural Organization). 1993. *World Education Report 1993.* Paris.

van der Gaag, Jacques, Elene Makonnen, and Pierre Englebert. 1991. "Trends in Social Indicators and Social Sector Financing." Policy Research Working Paper 662. World Bank, Washington, D.C.

World Bank. 1989. *Adjustment Lending: An Evaluation of Ten Years of Experience.* Policy and Research Series 1. Country Economics Department. Washington, D.C.

_____. 1990a. *Adjustment Lending Policies for Sustainable Growth.* Policy and Research Series 14. Country Economics Department. Washington, D.C.

_____. 1990b. *Social Indicators of Development 1990.* Baltimore: Johns Hopkins University Press.

_____. 1990c. *World Development Report 1990.* New York: Oxford University Press.

_____. 1991. *World Development Report 1991.* New York: Oxford University Press.

_____. 1992. *Adjustment Lending Policies for Sustainable Growth.* Policy and Research Series 22. Country Economics Department. Washington, D.C.

_____. 1993a. *Governance and Development.* Washington, D.C.

_____. 1993b. *The East Asian Miracle: Economic Growth and Public Policy.* A World Bank Policy Research Report. New York: Oxford University Press.

_____. 1993c. *Implementing the World Bank's Strategy to Reduce Poverty: Progress and Challenges.* Washington, D.C.

_____. 1993d. *Sustaining Rapid Development in East Asia and the Pacific.* Washington, D.C.

_____. 1993e. *World Development Report 1993: Investing in Health.* New York: Oxford University Press.

_____. 1994a. *Adjustment in Africa: Reforms, Results, and the Road Ahead.* A World Bank Policy Research Report. New York: Oxford University Press.

_____. 1994b. *Annual Report 1994.* Washington, D.C.

_____. 1994c. *Enhancing Women's Participation in Economic Development.* A World Bank Policy Paper. Washington, D.C.

_____. 1994d. "Investing in People.: Human Resources Development and Operations Policy, Office of the Vice President. Washington, D.C.

_____. 1994e. "The World Bank and Participation." Report of the Bankwide Learning Group on Participatory Development. Operations Policy Department. Washington, D.C.